Study Guide

Global Economic Issues and Policies

Joseph P. Daniels
Marquette University

David D. VanHoose
Baylor University

Prepared by

Norman C. Miller
Miami University (Ohio)

THOMSON

SOUTH-WESTERN

Australia · Canada · Mexico · Singapore · Spain · United Kingdom · United States

THOMSON

SOUTH-WESTERN

Study Guide to accompany

Global Economic Issues and Policies, 1e

Joseph P. Daniels and David D. VanHoose

Prepared by Norman C. Miller

Vice President, Editorial Director:
Jack W. Calhoun

Vice President, Editor-in-Chief:
Michael P. Roche

Publisher of Economics:
Michael B. Mercier

Acquisitions Editor:
Michael W. Worls

Senior Developmental Editor:
Jan Lamar

Senior Marketing Manager:
Janet Hennies

Production Editor:
Daniel C. Plofchan

Manufacturing Coordinator:
Sandee Milewski

Sr. Media Technology Editor:
Vicky True

Media Developmental Editor:
Peggy Buskey

Media Production Editor:
Pam Wallace

Design Project Manager:
Rik Moore

Cover Designer:
Rik Moore

Cover Photographer/Illustration:
PhotoDisc®, Inc.

Compositor:
Laurel Wood

Printer:
Victor Graphics
Baltimore, MD

Book ISBN: 0-324-17075-0

CONTENTS

CHAPTER ONE

Introduction to the Global Economy

Chapter Overview

Globalization refers to the increasing interconnectedness of people around the world, and the interdependence of economies, governments, and environments. There is no clear cut method for measuring the degree of globalization, but the volume of trade in goods and services as well as the volume of international capital flows (both relative to the size of a nation's economy) are two important aspects of globalization that can be measured. The volume of world trade has experienced a five-fold increase since 1979, and the volume of international capital flows appears to have increased even faster. The most globalized economies are small countries such as Ireland, Switzerland, Singapore, the Netherlands, Sweden, Canada, etc. The U.S., UK, and Germany are moderately globalized.

The increased degree of globalization in recent decades has been controversial. Proponents of globalization argue that specialization and trade serve to increase productive efficiency, which, in turn, raises the outputs and average standards of living of globalized nations. Furthermore, the free movement of funds internationally tends to allocate these funds to their most productive uses, thereby increasing world output optimally. Finally, they also point out that countries that are more highly globalized tend to have more civil liberties and political rights, and less corruption.

Opponents of globalization say that the correlations given in the previous sentence do not prove anything. That is, it is true that: (a) countries who have more civil liberties and political rights as well as less corruption tend: (b) to be more globalized. However, this correlation does not prove that (b) causes (a). The correlation could just be a coincidence. Furthermore, it is conceivable that (a) causes (b), i.e., countries with much political freedom and civil rights as well as less corruption might be more likely to do what is best for the country (rather than what is best for the rich and powerful). In this case, such countries might be more likely to pass laws that encourage globalization.

Opponents also argue that globalization tends to widen the distribution of income. That is, the rich gain and the poor either suffer or gain less than the rich. Opponents also contend that the firms of affluent nations take advantage of the workers in poorer countries and worsen the environment of the poorer countries. They point out, for example, that U.S. firms pay a wage rate to the workers in poor nations that is far below what is paid in America. Proponents of globalization counter by saying that these low wages are usually higher than what the workers could earn by working for the domestic firms.

A demand curve depicts the relationship between price and the quantity of a product demanded. The "law of demand" is that a lower price increases the quantity demanded. If anything alters the amount of a good that people want to buy at any given price, this is called either and increase in demand or a decrease in demand. An increase in demand represents a shift to the right in the demand curve. A decrease in demand represents a shift to the left in the demand curve. There are many events that can shift a demand curve. Some of the most salient are: variations in income, changes in preferences, or prices in other goods.

A supply curve shows the relationship between price and the quantity of a product supplied. The "law of supply" is that a higher price increases the quantity supplied. If anything alters the amount a good that people want to sell at any given price, this is called an increase in supply (if the supply curve shifts to the right) or a decrease in supply (if the supply curve shifts to the left). Some of the events that can shift a supply curve are: changes in the costs of resources that are used to produce the good, advances in technology, an increase or decrease in the number of sellers, variations in taxes or production subsidies, and changes in the prices of related goods and services.

Market equilibrium exists when the price is such that the quantity demanded equals the quantity supplied, as at point A in Figure 1, where the equilibrium price is P and the equilibrium quantity bought and sold is Q. If, by chance, the price falls below equilibrium, such as P', then the quantity demanded at point B exceeds the quantity supplied at point C. Therefore, when the price is P' there exists an excess demand (or a shortage) equal to the distance CB. If no international trade is permitted, then this shortage will induce sellers to increase the price until the market returns to equilibrium at point A. However, if international trade occurs, and if the home country can import this product at a price of P', then the shortage will be eliminated by imports. That is, in this situation the quantity of imports equals the distance CB. For example, if the U.S. produces 11 million cars in a year when Americans demand 16 million cars, then the U.S. will import 5 million cars.

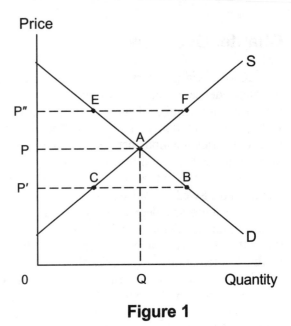

On the other hand, if the price rises above its equilibrium value, such as at P'' in Figure 1, then the quantity demanded at point E is less than the quantity supplied at point F. In this case, the excess supply (or surplus) equals the distance EF. If no international trade takes place, this surplus will prompt sellers to lower the price until the market returns to equilibrium

Figure 1

at point A. On the other hand, if the home country can export this product at a price of P'', then the surplus of EF is eliminated via exports. That is, the quantity of exports equals the distance EF. For example, if the U.S. produces 100 million tons of wheat, but Americans demand only 80 million tons, then U.S. exports of wheat will equal 20 million tons.

At each point on a demand curve, the height of the curve indicates the maximum that someone is willing to pay for that quantity of the good. In Figure 2, the market equilibrium price is $10, but there are consumers at each point on the demand curve who are willing to pay more than $10. For example, at point B someone is willing to pay approximately $15 for this good. Since they have to pay only $10, they obtain a "consumer's surplus" of $5. Similarly, at point C someone is willing to pay $12 for this good. Since they pay only $10, they obtain a consumer's surplus of $2. If we sum all of the individual consumers' surpluses in this graph, we obtain the "total consumers' surplus," which equals the area of triangle PBA. Since this area is (1/2) x (base) x (height) of the triangle, the total consumers' surplus equals (1/2) x (20) x (5) = $50. This indicates the dollar value of the total gains to consumers from buying 20 units of this good at a price of $10 each.

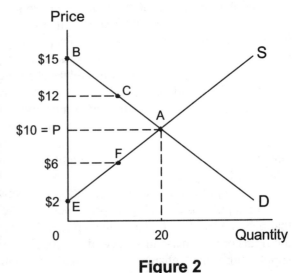

Figure 2

Sellers' surplus is an equivalent measure of the gains to sellers or producers. Each point on a supply curve indicates the minimum price that someone will accept for some quantity of the product. For example, at point E in Figure 2 a producer will accept approximately $2 for the good, but is able to sell it at the market price of $10. Thus, this seller experiences a seller's surplus of $8. Similarly, at point F there is a producer who is willing to sell for a price of $6. Since they are able to sell for $10, they obtain a producer's surplus of $4. The total producers' surplus is given by the area of the triangle EPA in Figure 2. This is equal to (1/2) x (base) x (height) = (1/2) x (20) x (8) = $80. This indicates the dollar value of the total gains to sellers or producers from selling 20 units of this good at a price of $10 each. The sum of total consumers' plus producers' surpluses in Figure 2 is $130.

Key Terms and Concepts

Capital flows
Consumers' surplus
Economic integration
Excess quantity demanded
Excess quantity supplied
Exports
Financial sector
Foreign direct investment
Foreign exchange market
Globalization
Imports
Law of demand
Law of supply
Market clearing price
Market demand
Market equilibrium
Market supply
Producers' surplus
Real sector

Multiple-Choice Questions

1. Which country is likely to be less globalized?
    a. Canada
    b. Finland
    c. Singapore
    d. Japan
    e. All of the above are likely to be equally globalized.

2. Globalization relates to increasing
    a. interconnectedness of people.
    b. trade in goods and services among nations.
    c. capital flows among nations.
    d. interdependence of governments and environments.
    e. all of the above

3.   The African Growth and Opportunity Act of 2000
      a.   increased the quota for emigration of Africans into the U.S.
      b.   provided funds for the education of African Americans.
      c.   eliminated the duties on nearly all goods produced in sub-Saharan Africa.
      d.   provided funds to subsidize businesses in sub-Saharan Africa.
      e.   both c and d

4.   The degree of globalization appears to be
      a.   positively correlated with political rights.
      b.   negatively correlated with corruption.
      c.   negatively correlated with civil liberties.
      d.   all of the above
      e.   both a and b

5.   Proponents of globalization maintain that it
      a.   enhances democracy.
      b.   increases productivity and world output.
      c.   reduces income inequalities.
      d.   all of the above
      e.   a and b

6.   Opponents of globalization maintain that it
      a.   allows the firms of advanced countries to abuse workers in poor nations.
      b.   reduces democracy.
      c.   increases income inequalities.
      d.   all of the above
      e.   a and c

7.   Capital flows relate to the sale of
      a.   services internationally.
      b.   merchandise internationally.
      c.   assets internationally.
      d.   all of the above
      e.   a and c

8.   Since 1979 global trade has
      a.   doubled.
      b.   tripled.
      c.   increased four-fold.
      d.   increased five-fold.
      e.   none of the above

9.   Since 1979 the volume of foreign exchange market transactions has
      a.   increased more rapidly than the volume of trade.
      b.   increased about five-fold.
      c.   tripled.
      d.   stayed about the same.
      e.   decreased slightly.

10. When the price of pizza falls from $2 per slice to $1.50 per slice, people want to buy more pizza. This illustrates
    a. the law of demand.
    b. an increase in quantity demanded.
    c. an increase in demand.
    d. all of the above
    e. a and b

11. When the price of a used economics textbook rises from $10 to $15, more students want to sell their book. This illustrates
    a. the law of supply.
    b. an increase in quantity supplied.
    c. an increase in supply.
    d. all of the above
    e. a and b

12. If cheap hamburgers are an inferior good, then what will happen to the demand curve for cheap hamburgers if everyone's income rises?
    a. It shifts to the right.
    b. It shifts to the left.
    c. It becomes vertical
    d. It becomes horizontal
    e. It is impossible to determine.

13. If double-decker bacon cheeseburgers are a normal good, then what will happen to the demand curve for them if everyone's income rises?
    a. It shifts to the right.
    b. It shifts to the left.
    c. It becomes vertical
    d. It becomes horizontal
    e. It is impossible to determine.

14. In the graph to the right, what are the values for the equilibrium price and quantity?
    a. P = 5 and Q = 20
    b. P = 8 and Q = 5
    c. P = 4 and Q = 25
    d. P = 8 and Q = 5
    e. P = 4 and Q = 15

15. What is the value for total consumers' surplus when the market is in equilibrium in #14?
    a. 100
    b. 80
    c. 50
    d. 30
    e. none of the above

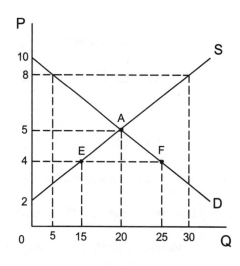

16. What is the value for total producers' surplus when the market is in equilibrium in #14?
    a. 100
    b. 80
    c. 50
    d. 30
    e. none of the above

17. What is the situation in the market in #14 if the price is $8?
    a. a surplus of 25
    b. a shortage of 25
    c. a surplus of 15
    d. a shortage of 15
    e. none of the above

18. What is the situation in the market in #14 if the price is $4?
    a. a surplus of 25
    b. a shortage of 5
    c. a surplus of 20
    d. a shortage of 10
    e. none of the above

19. If international trade occurs at a price of $8 in #14, then what is true?
    a. imports = 30
    b. exports = 25
    c. imports = 10
    d. exports = 10
    e. none of the above

20. If international trade occurs at a price of $4 in #14, then what is true?
    a. imports = 15
    b. exports = 15
    c. imports = 10
    d. exports = 10
    e. none of the above

Short-Answer Questions

1. What is meant by "globalization"?

2. What is the difference between the "real" sector and the "financial sector"?

3. What is bought and sold in the foreign exchange market?

4. Give two arguments of those who oppose globalization.

5. How can a country consistently produce more of a good than is consumed domestically?

6. In plain English, why does consumers' surplus measure the gain to consumers from buying a good?

7.   In plain English, why does producers' surplus measure the gain to producers from selling a good?

8.   Give two arguments of those who favor globalization.

9.   Why, logically, does the price in a market rise if the current price is below the equilibrium value?

10. How can a country consume more of a good than it produces domestically?

CHAPTER TWO

Comparative Advantage — How Nations Can Gain from International Trade

Chapter Overview

All countries have a limited amount of resources. This means that an increase in the production of any good, say good X, requires a decrease in the output of at least one other good, say good Y, because resources will have to be taken away from the Y industry in order to be used in the X industry. A graph that shows the maximum combinations of any two goods, X and Y, that a country is capable of producing is called a "production possibilities frontier," PPF. The slope of the PPF, which is a (−) number, indicates the decrease in Y divided by the increase in X as the economy moves down and to the right along its PPF. The absolute value of this slope, which is a (+) number, measures the opportunity cost of X, i.e., how much Y must be given up to produce an extra unit of X. This opportunity cost of X increases as progressively more X is produced (i.e., as the economy moves down and to the right along its PPF) because the resources released by the contracting Y industry will not be ideal for producing good X.

A country, say the U.S., has an absolute advantage in any good X if we can produce more of this good with any given amount of resources than can be produced by another country. This absolute advantage also means that the U.S. can produce X at a lower cost and, hence, the price of X will be lower in the U.S. than it is abroad. A country gains by trading along absolute advantage lines for two reasons. Consumers gain if they can import products at a lower price. Also, home firms (and their workers) gain if they can export products at prices in world markets that exceed the prices at home. From another perspective, world output rises (thereby making it possible for all nations to be better off) if all countries specialize in the production of goods wherein they are more productive (with any given amount of resources) than other countries.

A country can become better off if it engages in international trade even if it has an absolute advantage in all goods. This is known as the "theory of comparative advantage." A country has a comparative advantage in good X if it can produce X for a lower opportunity cost than in another country. The logic is as follows. Suppose that with a given amount of resources the U.S. can produce more of goods X and Y than another county, say Mexico. In this case, the U.S. has an absolute advantage in both X and Y. However, assume that the opportunity cost of 1 more unit of X is 3Y in the U.S. and 5Y in Mexico. In this example, the U.S. has a comparative advantage in good X. This means that we should produce more X and export it to Mexico. If Mexico is willing to pay us 4Y for each X that we sell them, then we gain 1Y from the transaction, because we must give up producing 3Y in order to produce the extra unit of X.

Why does it also pay the U.S. to import good Y from Mexico, even though (by assumption) we have an absolute advantage in Y? To understand this, note that if the opportunity cost of an extra X in the U.S. is 3Y, then the opportunity cost of an extra Y in the U.S. is 1/3X. Also, the opportunity cost of an extra unit of X is Mexico is 5Y. Thus, the opportunity cost of one more unit of Y in Mexico is 1/5X. Consequently, Mexico has a lower opportunity cost for Y than in U.S., i.e., Mexico has a comparative advantage in Y. The U.S. will be better off if it buys good Y from Mexico for, say, 1/4X for every unit of Y that we import. Why? Because, domestically if we want one more unit of Y, we must reduce our output of X by 1/3 of a unit. However, if we import 1Y from Mexico and have to pay only 1/4X, this, clearly, is cheaper than giving up 1/3X domestically.

If international trade allows countries to have more of all goods (and, hence, increase the average standard of living within all countries), then why is there so much controversy with regard to trade? The reason is that international trade redistributes income within a country. The incomes of some people increase, but the incomes of others decrease. The fact that trade raises the average standard of living within a country implies that the losers from trade lose less than the winners gain. Nevertheless, those who are worse-off from trade have, at times, been very vocal. Later chapters will explore this important issue.

Key Terms and Concepts

Absolute advantage
Autarky
Capital
Comparative advantage
Consumption possibilities
Contract manufacturing
Economic growth
Factors of production
Factor price equalization theorem
Factor proportions approach
Gains from trade
Heckscher-Ohlin theorem
Human capital
Leontief paradox
Magnification principle
Opportunity cost
Outscouring
Production possibilities frontier
Redistributive effects of trade
Relatively capital-abundant nation
Relatively capital-intensive good
Relatively labor-abundant nation
Relatively labor-intensive good
Rybczynski theory

Multiple-Choice Questions

1. Absolute advantage means that a country can produce
    a.   a good at a lower opportunity cost than in another country.
    b.   more of a good (with a given amount of resources) than another country.
    c.   a good at a lower dollar cost than another country.
    d.   all of the above
    e.   both b and c

2. Comparative advantage means that a country can produce
    a.   a good at a lower opportunity cost than in another country.
    b.   more of a good (with a given amount of resources) than another country.
    c.   a good at a lower dollar cost than another country.
    d.   all of the above
    e.   both b and c

3.   In the table below, what is the opportunity cost of the 2nd unit of X?

X	0	1	2	3
Y	8	7	5	0

    a.   1Y
    b.   2Y
    c.   3Y
    d.   4Y
    e.   5Y

4.   In the table for #1, what is the opportunity cost of the 1st unit of X?
    a.   1Y
    b.   2Y
    c.   3Y
    d.   4Y
    e.   5Y

5.   In the table for #1, what is the opportunity cost of the 7th unit of Y if output goes from 5Y to 7Y?
    a.   1/2X
    b.   1/3X
    c.   1X
    d.   1/5X
    e.   none of the above

6.   In the table below, which country has an absolute advantage in good X if both the U.S. and UK can produce the given quantities of X and Y with the same fixed number of resources?

	Good X	Good Y
U.S.	50 units	25 units
UK	30 units	10 units

    a.   the U.S.
    b.   the UK
    c.   impossible to determine

7.   In the table for #4, which country has an absolute advantage in good Y if both the U.S. and UK can produce the given quantities of X and Y with the same fixed number of resources?
    a.   the U.S.
    b.   the UK
    c.   impossible to determine

8.   In the table below, what is the opportunity cost of guns in the U.S.?

	Guns	Butter
U.S.	$100	$50
Canada	$200	$40

    a.   2 butter
    b.   5 butter
    c.   3 butter
    d.   1/2 butter
    e.   1/5 butter

9.   In the table in #8, what is the opportunity cost of guns in Canada?
     a.   2 butter
     b.   5 butter
     c.   3 butter
     d.   1/2 butter
     e.   1/5 butter

10. In the table in #8, which country has a comparative advantage in guns?
     a.   U.S.
     b.   Canada
     c.   impossible to determine

11. In the table in #8, what is the opportunity cost of butter in the U.S.?
     a.   2 guns
     b.   4 guns
     c.   1/2 gun
     d.   1/5 gun
     e.   none of the above

12. In the table in #8, what is the opportunity cost of butter in Canada?
     a.   2 guns
     b.   4 guns
     c.   1/2 gun
     d.   1/5 gun
     e.   none of the above

13. In the table in #8, which country has a comparative advantage in butter?
     a.   U.S.
     b.   Canada
     c.   impossible to determine

14. In the case given by the table in #8, if trade takes place along comparative advantage lines between the U.S. and Canada at a ratio of 3 butter per 1 gun, or 1/3 gun per butter, then how much does the U.S. gain if it produces one more unit of its export good and sells this to Canada?
     a.   1 butter
     b.   1/3 butter
     c.   0.20 butter
     d.   1/2 butter
     e.   none of the above

15. If the U.S. and Canada trade along comparative advantage lines in #8, then how much does Canada gain if i exports one unit of its comparative advantage good to the U.S. at a ratio of 3 butter per gun or 1/3 gun per butter?
     a.   1 gun
     b.   1/2 gun
     c.   20 guns
     d.   2 guns
     e.   none of the above

16.   Which of the following statements is not true?
    a.   Specialization along comparative advantage lines increases world output.
    b.   Specialization and trade along comparative advantage lines can make all countries better off.
    c.   Specialization and trade along comparative advantage lines helps everyone within a country.
    d.   Exports are always good and imports are always bad.
    e.   c and d

17.   In the graph to the right, which point has the highest opportunity cost for good X?
    a.   A
    b.   B
    c.   C
    d.   D

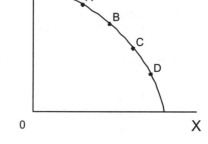

18.   The economy is at point B in autarky in the graph for #17 with an opportunity cost of X equal to 5Y. If this country can trade in world market at a ratio of 3Y per X, then in which good does this country have a comparative advantage?
    a.   good X
    b.   good Y
    c.   impossible to determine

19.   In #18, in which direction will the economy move when it specializes along comparative advantage lines?
    a.   toward point A
    b.   toward points C and D
    c.   impossible to determine

20.   Why is the idea of free trade so controversial?
    a.   Because only the rich nations gain from trade.
    b.   Because only the poor nations gain from trade.
    c.   Because trade always harms some groups within each country.
    d.   both a and b
    e.   both b and c

Short-Answer Questions

1.   Why is there an opportunity cost for producing more of any good?

2.   What is a Production Possibilities Frontier, PPF?

3.   What is the economic significance of the slope of a PPF?

4.   Why does the opportunity cost of X increase as progressively more X is produced?

5.   What is the meaning of "absolute advantage"?

6.   Why will a country gain if it trades along absolute advantage lines?

7.   What is the meaning of "comparative advantage"?

8.   Why will a country gain if it specializes and trades along comparative advantage lines?

9.   Why is the subject of international trade so controversial?

10.   Why does it pay a country to engage in international trade even if it has an absolute advantage in all goods?

CHAPTER THREE

Sources of Comparative Advantage

Chapter Overview

We know from Chapter 2 that a country will have a comparative advantage in a good, say good X, if it has a lower opportunity cost in autarky that exists in another country. The obvious question is, "what can cause autarky opportunity costs to differ?" This chapter focuses on how differences in the endowments of resources (or factors of production) can create comparative advantage. This theory of comparative advantage is called the "Heckscher-Ohlin" theorem after the two men who began its development early in the 20th century.

Begin with two important definitions. First, a country is **relatively capital abundant** if the ratio of its capital stock, K, to its labor supply, L, exceeds the capital to labor ratio in another country. For example, if the U.S. has a capital stock of 1000 and only 50 workers, then the ratio $(K/L)_{US} = 1000/50 = 20$. On the other hand, if the capital stock in Canada is 400 and the labor supply is 40, then the ratio $(K/L)_{Can} = 400/40 = 10$. In this example, the U.S. is the relatively capital abundant country. That is, we have more capital per worker than Canada. If the (K/L) ratios are inverted, this gives the labor to capital ratios. Our example yields: $(L/K)_{US} = 1/20$ and $(L/K)_{Can} = 1/10$. Since 1/10 is larger than 1/20, it follows that Canada is the relatively labor abundant country.

Good X is **relatively capital intensive** compared to good Y if the ratio of capital to labor needed to produce a unit of X exceeds that for good Y. For example, suppose that it take 30 units of capital for every worker in the X industry, but only 5 units of capital per worker in the Y industry. Then $(Kx/Lx) = 30/1$ and this exceeds $(Ky/Ly) = 5/1$. In this case, we can also say that good Y is the relatively labor intensive product.

The Heckscher-Ohlin theorem is as follows. If a country, say the U.S., is relatively capital abundant compared to another country, say Canada, then the U.S. will have a lower opportunity cost in autarky for the relatively capital intensive good (say X) and Canada will have a lower opportunity cost in autarky for the relatively labor intensive good (say Y). That is, a country with much capital compared to labor will have a comparative advantage in capital intensive goods, and a country with much labor compared to capital will have a comparative advantage in labor intensive goods.

The Heckscher-Ohlin theorem is illustrated in Figure 3. The solid PPF represents the U.S. If the U.S. has much capital and if good X is capital intensive, then we will be able to produce more X than Y. This gives a relatively flat PPF for the U.S. Recall that the absolute value of the slope of the PPF is the opportunity cost of X. If the U.S. autarky point is somewhere near the middle of its PPF such as point A, then the relatively flat slope at point A means that the U.S. has a relatively low opportunity cost of X.

The dashed PPF in Figure 3 corresponds to Canada. If it has a relative abundance of labor and if good Y is labor intensive, then Canada will be able to produce more of good Y than X. This yields a relatively steep PPF, which, in turn, implies that the absolute value for the slope of the PPF in

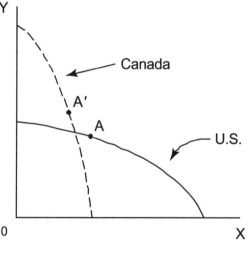

Figure 3

14

autarky (such as at point A') will be a relatively large number. In other words, Canada will have a relatively high opportunity cost for good X in autarky. Therefore, the U.S. has a comparative advantage in X (the capital intensive good) and Canada has a comparative advantage in Y (the labor intensive good) just as the Heckscher-Ohlin theorem concludes.

In the early 1950s Wassily Leontief tested the Heckscher-Ohlin theorem using data for the U.S. economy. He calculated the ratio of the capital compared to the amount of labor used to produce U.S. exports. Call this $(K/L)_{Ex}$. Also, he calculated the capital to labor ratio used to produce U.S. imports, $(K/L)_{Im}$. At that time in history the U.S. clearly was the most capital abundant country in the world. Hence, the Heckscher-Ohlin theorem predicted that the U.S. would export relatively capital intensive products. However, Leontief found that just the opposite was true. That is, $(K/L)_{Ex} < (K/L)_{Im}$. This result is called the **Leontief paradox**.

The Leontief paradox stimulated much research. Now we know that Leontief's conclusion can be reversed if we take account of the skills and knowledge embedded in U.S. exports and imports. To explain, U.S. exports at that time used relatively more labor than did U.S. imports. However, the labor used to produce exports was highly skilled labor, while the labor used to produce imports was relatively unskilled. Economists have calculated a dollar value for the skills and knowledge embodied in labor inputs. This is called "human capital" When the values of human capital needed to produce U.S. exports and U.S. imports are added to the values for nonhuman capital needed to produce each type of good, the result is that U.S. exports become relatively capital intensive compared to U.S. imports. Thus, the Leontief paradox is solved.

The Heckscher-Ohlin theorem has several important corollaries that deal with the distribution of income. One of these corollaries is called the **Stolper-Samuelson** theorem, which says that international trade along comparative advantage lines in a manner that is consistent with the Heckscher-Ohlin theorem will increase the incomes of some resources and lower the incomes of other resources within each country. For example, assume that the U.S., is relatively capital abundant and, hence, exports the capital intensive good, say good X. In this case, capital (which is used intensively in our export industry) will experience an increase in its earnings while labor here (which is used intensively in the industry that competes with imports) will experience a decrease in income.

Figure 4 helps to explain the Stolper-Samuelson theorem. The PPF relates to the U.S., who is assumed to have a comparative advantage in X, the relatively capital intensive good. If production in autarky occurs at point A, then a comparative advantage in good X will shift resources away from the Y industry and into the X industry as the economy moves down and to the right from A toward, say, point B.

When industry Y contracts it releases some capital but much labor, because (by assumption) good Y is relatively labor intensive. On the other hand, when

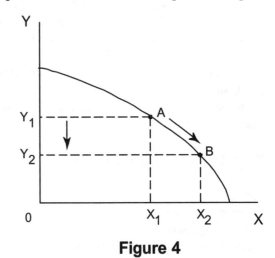

Figure 4

industry X expands, it needs much capital but only a relatively small amount of labor. Since industry Y has released much labor, it follows that an excess supply of labor will arise. Consequently, wage rates will fall in order for all workers to find a job. This decrease in the wage rate permanently lowers the incomes of labor (which is the resource used intensively in the import competing Y industry).

On the other hand, the expanding X industry needs much capital, but only a little capital is released by the contracting Y industry. Hence, a shortage of capital will arise, and this will increase the incomes of owners of capital. (Economists refer to the payment to capital as "rent.") The increase in rent is permanent. Therefore, specialization along Heckscher-Ohlin lines permanently raises the income of capital owners and permanently lowers the incomes of labor in the country whose comparative advantage is in the capital intensive product. The Stolper-Samuelson theorem provides a good reason why free trade is controversial, i.e., some resources will have their incomes lowered permanently.

A second corollary of the Heckscher-Ohlin theory is called the **factor price equalization theorem**, which says that free trade will move wage rates at home and abroad toward each other, and will tend to equalize rents (the payment to owners of capital) internationally. To see this, assume that Mexico is a relatively labor abundant country and the U.S. is relatively capital abundant. Also, let X be the capital intensive good and Y be labor intensive. Hence, according to the Heckscher-Ohlin theorem, the U.S. has a comparative advantage in X, and Mexico's comparative advantage is in Y.

The Stolper-Samuelson theorem says that in this situation wage rates in the U.S. will fall and rental rates (the payments to capital) will rise. Just the opposite takes place in Mexico. When Mexico increases the output of Y (their comparative advantage good) they need much labor, but only a relatively small amount of labor is released when the output of X decreases in Mexico. Thus, a labor shortage arises, and this permanently increases wage rates in Mexico. However, their expanding Y industry requires only a relatively small amount of capital, but their contracting X industry releases much capital. This creates a surplus of capital in Mexico, thereby permanently lowering rental rates on capital.

The upshot of all this is as follows. Wage rates are initially high in the U.S. because, by assumption, the U.S. has relatively a small amount of labor. The high wage rates in the U.S. fall when we specialize and trade. Initially, wage rates are low in Mexico, because of their relative abundance of labor. Specialization and trade along comparative lines that is consistent with the Heckscher-Ohlin theory serves to raise wage rates there. Therefore, the wage rates in the two countries tend to approach each other. A similar conclusion holds for rental rates on capital.

Finally, the **Rybczynski theorem** states that if prices are held constant then an increase in the endowment of one resource, say capital, will increase the output of the capital intensive good, say X, and decrease the output of the labor intensive good, say Y. Thus, if an economy grows via an increase in the supply of its relatively abundant resource, then the output of its comparative advantage good rises and the output of its imported good falls. Both of these events tend to increase the home country's comparative advantage in X and enhance international trade. Contrastingly, if the home country grows via an increase in the endowment of its relatively scarce resource (say labor), then the output of the good, say Y, that uses this resource intensively will rise and the output of the other good, X, will fall. Such economic growth reduces the comparative advantage in X and decreases the amount of international trade.

Key Terms and Concepts

Capital
Contract manufacturing
Economic growth
Factor price equalization theorem
Factors of production
Heckscher-Ohlin theorem
Human capital
Leontief paradox
Magnification principle
Outsourcing
Relatively capital-abundant country
Relatively capital-intensive good
Relatively labor-abundant country

Relatively labor-intensive good
Rybczynski theorem
Stolper-Samuelson theorem
Value added

Multiple-Choice Questions

1. The term "relative factor endowments" refers to the ratio of
    a. capital to labor needed to produce each good.
    b. capital to labor in each country.
    c. wages to rental rates in each country.
    d. the price of X to the price of Y in each country.
    e. none of the above

2. The term "relative factor intensities" refers to the ratio of
    a. capital to labor needed to produce each good.
    b. capital to labor in each country.
    c. wages to rental rates in each country.
    d. the price of X to the price of Y in each country.
    e. none of the above

3. The Heckscher-Ohlin theorem deals with a reason for comparative advantage based on differences in
    a. home versus foreign preferences.
    b. home versus foreign technologies.
    c. home versus foreign endowments of resources.
    d. differences in the size of the home versus foreign economies.
    e. none of the above

4. If the U.S. has 1000 units of capital and 200 units of labor, while Mexico has 50 units of capital and 100 units of labor, then
    a. the U.S. is relatively capital abundant.
    b. the U.S. is relatively labor abundant.
    c. Mexico is relative labor abundant.
    d. a and c
    e. b and c

5. If it takes 6 units of capital per worker to produce each unit of X, and 2 units of capital per worker to produce each unit of Y, then
    a. X is the relatively capital intensive good.
    b. Y is the relatively capital intensive good.
    c. X is the relatively labor intensive good.
    d. Y is the relatively labor intensive good.
    e. a and d

6. If the facts given in #4 and #5 are used, then according to the Heckscher-Ohlin theorem,
    a. Mexico has a comparative advantage in X.
    b. Mexico has a comparative advantage in Y.
    c. the U.S. has a comparative advantage in X.
    d. b and c
    e. a and b

7.   If the facts given in #4 and #5 are used, then which good will each country import?
     a.   The U.S. imports Y.
     b.   Mexico imports X.
     c.   The U.S. imports X.
     d.   Mexico imports Y.
     e.   a and b

8.   If the facts given in #4 and #5 are used, then which groups will be in favor of international trade?
     a.   labor in the U.S.
     b.   labor in Mexico
     c.   capitalists in the U.S.
     d.   capitalists in Mexico
     e.   b and c

9.   The Leontief paradox refers to the fact that
     a.   the U.S. exported products that used almost no capital
     b.   the U.S. exported products that used almost no labor.
     c.   U.S. exports used relatively more capital than our imports.
     d.   U.S. exports used relatively less capital than our imports.
     e.   none of the above

10. Economists have solved the Leontief paradox by
     a.   discovering mistakes in the data that he used.
     b.   rejecting the Heckscher-Ohlin theorem.
     c.   taking account of the human capital embodied in labor.
     d.   proving that technologies differ between countries.
     e.   none of the above

11. According to the Heckscher-Ohlin theorem, which of the following is true?
     a.   The autarky relative price of X will be lower if the home country has a relative abundance of the resource used intensively to produce X.
     b.   The income of the resource used intensively to produce a country's comparative advantage good will rise.
     c.   The income of the resource used intensively to produce the good that is imported will fall.
     d.   a, b, and c are all true
     e.   a, b, and c are all not true

12. If there are 20 workers, L, in the U.S. and each one has 20 units of capital, K, and if there are 4 workers in Canada and each one has 10 units of capital, then what are the K/L ratios in each country?
     a.   1 in the U.S. and 2.5 in Canada
     b.   1 in the U.S. and 10 in Canada
     c.   20 in the U.S. and 2.5 in Canada
     d.   20 in the U.S. and 10 in Canada
     e.   none of the above

13. If the facts in #12 are true, then which country has a comparative advantage in good X?
    a. Canada
    b. U.S.
    c. No one has a comparative advantage.
    d. It is impossible to determine with the given information.

14. If good X requires 25 units of capital per worker, while good Y requires 5 units of capital per worker, then which country has a comparative advantage in good Y in #12?
    a. Canada
    b. U.S.
    c. No one has a comparative advantage.
    d. It is impossible to determine with the given information.

15. If the facts in #12 and #14 are true, then who will be against international trade?
    a. labor in the U.S.
    b. labor in Canada
    c. owners of capital in the U.S.
    d. owners of capital in Canada
    e. a and d

16. According to the Rybczynski theorem, what will happen if the U.S. has a comparative advantage in a labor intensive good Y, and our labor force grows significantly while our capital stock remains unchanged?
    a. The output of Y increases and X decreases.
    b. The output of X increases and Y decreases.
    c. Our comparative advantage increases.
    d. Our comparative advantage decreases.
    e. a and c

17. What will happen in #16 with regard to international trade?
    a. The volume of trade increases.
    b. The volume of trade decreases.
    c. The volume of trade remains the same.
    d. It is impossible to determine with this information.

18. Assume that the U.S. exports products that use much skilled labor and imports products that use a great deal of unskilled labor. What is true according to the Heckscher-Ohlin theorem and its corollaries?
    a. Skilled labor in the U.S. will be against international trade.
    b. Skilled labor in the U.S. will be for international trade.
    c. Unskilled labor in the U.S. will be against international trade.
    d. both a and c
    e. both b and c

19. If the facts in #18 are true, then
    a. wages for skilled labor will rise in the U.S.
    b. wages for unskilled labor will fall in the U.S.
    c. the wages of U.S. unskilled labor will approach the wages of unskilled labor abroad.
    d. all of the above
    e. b and c

20.   Suppose that good Z is relatively capital intensive and good V is labor intensive. The U.S. and Japan trade along comparative advantage lines as determined via the Heckscher-Ohlin theorem, and the U.S. exports good V while Japan exports good Z. What is true?
      a.   The U.S. is relatively capital abundant.
      b.   Japan is relatively capital abundant.
      c.   Wage rates will rise in the U.S.
      d.   b and c
      e.   a and c

Short-Answer Questions

1.   What is meant by "human capital"?

2.   Briefly explain one way that the Leontief paradox was solved?

3.   State the Heckscher-Ohlin theorem as briefly as possible.

4.   What is the Stolper-Samuelson theorem?

5.   According to the Stolper-Samuelson theorem, which resource within a country will be harmed by international trade, and which resource gains?

6.   Define "value added."

7.   What is "economic growth"?

8.   What is the Rybczynski theorem?

9.   What is the difference between "relative capital abundant" and "relative capital intensive"?

10.   If a country is relatively labor abundant (compared to capital) and good X is relatively capital intensive (compared to good Y), then which good will the country export and which good will it import according to the Heckscher-Ohlin theorem?

CHAPTER FOUR

Regulating International Trade — Trade Policies and Their Effects

Chapter Overview

The chapter deals primarily with the effects of **tariffs** and **quotas** on international trade and on the well-being of the countries that utilize them. Since tariffs and quotas reduce international trade, they generally lower the wellbeing of the country that levies them. Calculation of the cost to consumers for every domestic job that is saved via tariffs and quotas suggests that these costs are extremely high.

First, however, the chapter reviews how a tax on a product, such as a domestic sales tax, affects the market for that product. Such a tax is collected from the seller, who then tries to pass it on to the consumer by adding the sales tax to the price of the product. However, usually the burden of the tax is shared (not necessarily equally) by the buyer and seller. Obviously, the tax is **shifted forward** because the consumer ends up paying a higher price after the tax is added to the pre-tax price. Less obviously, the seller also shares in the burden of the tax. This is called **backward shifting**, and it occurs because consumers buy a smaller quantity when they have to pay more for each unit after the tax is imposed. This decrease in the quantity demanded induces sellers to lower their before the tax price, at least slightly. Hence, even though consumers pay a higher price (including the tax), the sellers end up with less per unit after they give the government the tax revenue that they have collected on each unit sold.

A tariff is a tax on imports. There are: (a) **ad valorem** tariffs, which are a percentage of the value of the imports, (b) **specific** tariffs, which are a fixed amount on each unit of the good that is imported, and (c) **combination** tariffs, which utilize both (a) and (b). A small country is one that is too small to affect the international price of any good. A small country is always worse off when it levies an import tariff. Consumers lose because they must pay a higher price, and this reduces their **consumers' surplus**. However, a portion of the decrease in consumers' surplus goes to domestic producers of the good, who are better off because they can now charge a higher price (when imports cost more), and because they sell more. That portion of the loss to consumers that goes to domestic producers is called the **redistribution effect**.

Another portion of the decrease in consumers' surplus goes to the government in the form of **tariff revenue**. However, a portion of the loss in consumers' surplus does not go to anyone else. This portion of the loss is called the **deadweight loss** to society from the tariff. Logically, a country's level of wellbeing increases when it engages in international trade along comparative advantage lines. Therefore, when a tariff reduces the volume of international trade, it decreases the level of wellbeing within a small country.

A **large country** is one that is big enough to affect the market price of some or many goods in international markets. For example, if the U.S. were to decrease it demand for oil substantially, the price of oil would fall in world markets. It is possible for a large country to be better or worse off when it levies an import tariff. To explain, all of the effects in the previous two paragraphs continue to exist for a large country. In particular, a portion of the loss in consumers' surplus does not go either to domestic producers or the government. This loss is also called the deadweight loss from the tariff.

On the other hand, if, say, the U.S. government levied a high tariff on oil imports, then our demand for imports of oil would decrease and the price of oil in world markets would fall. Thus, the U.S. as a country would be able to buy oil in world markets at a lower price, even though U.S. consumers are paying a higher price after the tariff is added. This improvement in the U.S. terms of trade tends to increase the level of well-being for the U.S. The **net effect** of the tariff by a large country is this gain from a lower world price for our imports minus the deadweight loss mentioned above. The net effect could be positive or negative.

An import **quota** represents a policy that restricts the **quantity** of imports. An **absolute quota** is a quantitative amount of a product that can enter a country during a specified time interval, usually one year. A **tariff-rate quota** allows a specified quantity of a good to enter the country at a reduced tariff rate, but then the tariff rate rises for any quantity above the quota. The effects of a quota are very similar, but not identical, to the effects of a tariff.

When a small country levies an absolute quota it does not directly affect the price of the imported good. However, if home consumers wish to buy more of the imported good that is allowed by the quota, this will drive the price up until people want to import exactly the quantity allowed by the quota. When this happens, then home consumers are worse off because the higher price reduces their consumers' surplus. A portion of this, called the **redistribution effect**, goes to home producers who gain because they can now sell at a higher price.

In the case of an absolute quota, there is no tariff revenue. Thus, if the government gives foreigners the right to export into the home country, then the loss to society is larger than in the case of an equivalent tariff. This loss includes what was called the deadweight loss above, plus an amount that equals the value of the tariff revenue that could have been collected if the government had levied a tariff instead of imposing a quota. The latter is called the **quota rent**. This large loss in domestic wellbeing always occurs if the home government induces the foreign exporters to voluntarily restrict their exports to the home country, i.e. a voluntary export restraint or **VER**. If the home government is wise, then it will not give away the rights to export to the home country when it imposes a quota. Instead, it will auction-off the quota rights, and the revenue from this will greatly reduce the decrease in domestic wellbeing from the quota.

Dumping occurs when a foreign exporter sells its product here either: (a) at a lower price than it charges its home customers, or (b) at a price that is lower than its average cost per unit. Often, foreign firms dump their products here if their government **subsidizes** their exports. When a foreign firm engages in dumping, the home government is allowed to levy a **countervailing duty**, CVD, which is a tax in imports that offsets the subsidy that the foreign firm might be receiving from its government.

Key Terms and Concepts

Absolute quota
Ad valorem tariff
Backward shifted
Beggar-thy-neighbor policy
Combination tariff
Countervailing duty (CVD)
Deadweight loss
Dumping
Export subsidy
First best policy
Forward shifted
Import quota
Large country
Non-tariff barriers
Quota
Quota rent
Redistribution effect of a tariff

Second best policy
Small country
Specific tariff
Tariff
Tariff-rate quota
Voluntary export restraint (VER)

Multiple-Choice Questions

1. When the government levies a sales tax on a product, and collects the tax from the seller, then how does this affect the market for that product?
    a. The supply curve shifts down and to the right.
    b. The demand curve shifts up and to the right.
    c. The supply curve shifts up and to the left.
    d. The demand curve shifts down and to the left.
    e. c and d

2. Under normal circumstances the burden of a sales tax
    a. is paid entirely by the seller because the government collects the tax from them.
    b. is paid entirely by the buyer because the tax is added to the price.
    c. is paid partly by the buyer and partly by the seller.
    d. falls on those who pay an income tax.

3. What do we call a tax of a fixed amount per unit of imports?
    a. specific tariff
    b. ad valorem tariff
    c. combination tariff
    d. tariff-rate quota
    e. none of the above

4. Which of the following represents a tax on imports that is relatively low until a specific quantity of imports is bought, at which time the tax increases?
    a. specific tariff
    b. ad valorem tariff
    c. combination tariff
    d. tariff-rate quota
    e. none of the above

5. Which of the following represents a tax on imports that is a fixed percentage of the value of imports?
    a. specific tariff
    b. ad valorem tariff
    c. combination tariff
    d. tariff-rate quota
    e. none of the above

6.   Which of the following specifies the maximum quantity of a particular type of import?
        a.   specific tariff
        b.   ad valorem tariff
        c.   combination tariff
        d.   tariff-rate quota
        e.   none of the above

7.   What do we know for certain when a small country levies an import tariff on product X?
        a.   Consumers' surplus decreases.
        b.   Domestic producers of X are better off.
        c.   The country as a whole is worse off.
        d.   all of the above
        e.   both b and c

8.   What name is given to the decrease in consumers' surplus (when an import tariff is levied) that no one gains?
        a.   the redistribution effect
        b.   the tariff revenue
        c.   the deadweight loss
        d.   the quota rent
        e.   none of the above

9.   What is the gain to foreign exporters if they agree to a voluntary export restraint, VER?
        a.   the redistribution effect
        b.   the deadweight loss
        c.   the quota rent
        d.   forward shifting
        e.   none of the above

10.   Initially, the U.S. imports 100 units of product Y at a price of $5 each. Then the U.S. government levies a specific tariff of $10 per unit. This raises the price that home consumers pay for the product by the full amount of the tariff, and, thus, it decreases the quantity of Y demanded in the U.S. to 90. Home producers increase their price to equal the price of imports, and sell 20 more units than before the tariff. What is the new quantity of imports after the tariff?
        a.   90
        b.   110
        c.   120
        d.   70
        e.   It is impossible to determine this with the given amount of information.

11.   In #10, what is the total value for the government's tariff revenue?
        a. $900
        b. $110
        c. $1200
        d. $700
        e.   It is impossible to determine this with the given amount of information.

12. Use the information given in #10 to determine what value for an absolute quota for imports of good Y would yield an import price of $15.
    a. 70
    b. 90
    c. 55
    d. 110
    e. none of the above

13. Dumping occurs when foreign exporters
    a. sell excessively large amounts of their product at a high price.
    b. charge domestic consumers less than they charge their home customers.
    c. sell us their product at a loss.
    d. all of the above
    e. b and c

14. What is a countervailing duty?
    a. It is a tariff that matches the tariff that foreign countries have on our product.
    b. It is a task that our exporters perform in order to neutralize the harm from imports.
    c. It is a task that our import competing firms perform that counters the low price of imports.
    d. It is a tariff on imports that offsets the advantage given to foreign exporters when they are subsidized by their governments.
    e. none of the above

15. A VER refers to a
    a. very energetic reversal (of tariffs).
    b. velocity of energy reflection.
    c. voluntary export restraint.
    d. voluntary export relief.
    e. none of the above

16. What do we know about a VER versus an import tariff for a small country?
    a. They both reduce the level of domestic wellbeing.
    b. The VER reduces wellbeing more than the tariff.
    c. The tariff reduces wellbeing more than the VER.
    d. both a and b
    e. both a and c

17. When a large country levies an import tariff on a product that it usually imports heavily, then the
    a. large country is certain to be worse off.
    b. large country is certain to be better off.
    c. large country might be better or worse off.
    d. price of the product in world markets rises.
    e. c and d

18. What do we know about the effects on domestic wellbeing in a small country from an import tariff versus an equivalent (i.e., they both yield the same quantity of imports) absolute quota if the government auctions off the quota rights?
    a.   they are the equal
    b.   wellbeing decreases more with the quota
    c.   wellbeing decreases more with the tariff
    d.   there is no way to tell which one decreases wellbeing more

19. If a small country levies a 5% ad valorem tariff on imports of a product that sells for $40 in international markets, then what price will home consumers pay after the tariff is imposed?
    a. $45
    b. $42
    c. $42.50
    d.   impossible to determine

20. Suppose that a large country levies a 10% ad valorem tariff on imports of a product that typically sells for $100 in international markets, but when the quantity of home demand for imports falls (as a result of the tariff) the price in world markets falls to $90. What price will home consumers pay after the tariff is imposed?
    a. $100
    b. $110
    c. $109
    d. $99
    e.   none of the above

Short-Answer Questions

1.   What is forward shifting of a tax?

2.   What is an absolute quota?

3.   What happens to home consumers' surplus when a tariff is imposed on imports?

4.   What do we call the gain to home producers from a tariff that is part of the loss to home consumers?

5.   What type of tariff is a fixed percentage of the value of imports?

6.   What type of tariff is a fixed amount per unit imported plus a percentage of the value of imports?

7.   What is meant by the term "large country" within the context of international trade?

8.   What name is given to the revenue that the home government can gain if it auctions off the quota rights?

9.   What is dumping?

10. What can a country do if it is harmed by dumping?

CHAPTER FIVE

Regionalism and Multilateralism

Chapter Overview

This chapter examines levels of economic integration by countries from both a regional and a multilateral perspective. At the regional level a country can make **preferential trade arrangements** (with regard to specific products or on all products) with one or more countries. This can be done unilaterally or via negotiations with the other countries. Preferential trade arrangements can take many forms such reduced tariff rates or the relaxation of quotas.

A closer level of economic integration is a **free trade area**. The members of a free trade area, such as NAFTA, have zero tariffs and quotas for trade among themselves. However, each country within a free trade area may have whatever tariffs and/or quotas it desires for trade with nonmembers. This is not true for a **customs union**, which is a free trade area plus common (among the members of the customs union) tariffs and/or quotas with regard to trade involving nonmembers.

An even closer level of economic integration is a **common market**, which is defined as a customs union plus the free movement of resources (including financial capital) between its members. The EU was essentially a common market in the 1980s. Finally, an **economic union** is a common market plus the coordination of economic policies between its members. The EU is now an economic union.

The **trade concentration ratio** measures the extent of trade among the members of a trading bloc (e.g. a free trade area, or customs union, etc.) relative to trade between these members and the rest of the world. Formally, the trade concentration ratio for, say, NAFTA or any other trading bloc, is calculated by dividing (the percentage of NAFTA's trade that occurs between its members) by (the percentage of world trade that involves NAFTA countries).

NAFTA was established in 1994 between the U.S., Canada, and Mexico. Opponents of NAFTA predicted that it would cause a massive inflow of Mexican goods into the U.S. and a substantial movement of U.S. firms to Mexico. This has not happened. The most significant effects so far appear to be a large increase in U.S. exports to Mexico, and an increase in two-way trade between Canada and Mexico.

The reduction of trade barriers between two countries is not necessarily beneficial. For example, suppose that Germany initially has a tariff on imports of good X from all countries, and that initially Germany imports X from the U.S., because the U.S. is the low cost producer of X. Then let Germany enter into a free trade agreement with the UK. If the tariff free price of X from the UK is lower than the price that German consumers have to pay for imports of X from the U.S. (including the tariff), then Germany will switch and buy X only from the UK.

The lower price that German consumers pay for X from the UK increases consumers' surplus in Germany. Part of this increase represents a redistribution effect, because German firms who produce X are worse off when the imported price of X decreases. Another part of the increase in German consumers' surplus is offset by lost tariff revenue for the German government. However, a portion of the increase in German consumers' surplus is not a loss for anyone, and this gain is called **trade creation**.

On the other hand, in the example above, the country of Germany now buys X from the UK and pays them more for X than they were paying the U.S. Note that German consumers pay less for imports of X from the UK than they did when they imported from the U.S., because they had to pay a tariff on X from the U.S. However, even though the German consumers pay less for X from the UK, the country of Germany pays the UK more for X than it was paying the U.S., because the U.S. is the low cost producer here. The loss to the country of Germany, because it is paying the UK more for X than it was paying the U.S. is called **trade diversion**.

The net effect for Germany of the free trade agreement with the UK is plus trade creation minus trade diversion, and this could be positive (a net gain) or negative (a net loss). In general, a country should enter into free trade agreements with countries who are the low cost producers of the goods that will be imported. To this end, it is best to enter into free trade agreements with as many countries as possible, because this raises the probability that one of them will be the low cost producer for each good.

The last sentence implies that **multilateralism** (which is the reduction of trade barriers among all countries in the world) is the best approach. This idea is embodied in the GATT, which has established many rounds of tariff reductions among essentially all countries on a regular basis since WWII. An integral part of multilateralism is the concept of **most favored nation**, which means that when a country, say the U.S., reduces tariffs on any product from another country, say Japan, then all other countries who enjoy a most favored nation status (which usually means all but a handful of nations) automatically get the same tariff reductions.

In 1993 the members of GATT established the world trade organization, WTO, to administer and oversee the trade agreements that have been negotiated via GATT. If a country believes that one of its trading partners is engaging in unfair trade practices (such as dumping or subsidizing exports) or violating a trade agreement, then it can petition the WTO to investigate the matter. If the WTO decides that rules are being broken, it then gives the offended country permission to impose safeguard measures, including possibly high tariffs on products from the offending country.

Section 201 of the Trade Act of 1974 within the U.S., gives U.S. industries that are threatened with serious harm from imports the right to petition a federal government organization called the international trade commission, **ITC**, for relief in the form of tariffs, quotas, or subsidies. The ITC makes a recommendation to the president as to what should be done.

Key Terms and Concepts

Comment market
Customs union
Economic union
Free trade area
General Agreement of Tariffs and Trade, GATT
General Agreement on Trade in Services, GATS
Most favored nation
Multilateralism
Preferential trade arrangements
Regionalism
Rules of origin
Section 201
Trade concentration ratio
Trade creation
Trade deflection
Trade diversion
World Trade Organization, WTO

Multiple-Choice Questions

1. Which of the following refers to a trade agreement among a few countries?
    a.   multilateralism
    b.   trade creation
    c.   regionalism
    d.   trade diversion
    e.   none of the above

2. Which of the following refers to a trade agreement whereby all members have zero tariffs for trade with other members and common external tariffs, but no freedom of resource movements among the members?
    a.   free trade area
    b.   customs union
    c.   common market
    d.   economic union
    e.   none of the above

3. Which of the following refers to a trade agreement whereby all members have zero tariffs for trade with other members, but each member can have their own tariffs on every product when trading with nonmembers, and there is no freedom of resource movements among members?
    a.   free trade area
    b.   customs union
    c.   common market
    d.   economic union
    e.   none of the above

4. Which of the following refers to a trade agreement whereby all members have zero tariffs for trade with other members, all members have the same external tariffs, and resources can move freely among members?
    a.   free trade area
    b.   customs union
    c.   common market
    d.   economic union
    e.   none of the above

5. What is NAFTA?
    a.   free trade area
    b.   customs union
    c.   common market
    d.   economic union
    e.   none of the above

6. What is the European Union?
    a.   free trade area
    b.   customs union
    c.   common market
    d.   economic union
    e.   none of the above

7. What form of economic integration do the 50 states of the U.S. have with each other?
    a.   free trade area
    b.   customs union
    c.   common market
    d.   economic union
    e.   none of the above

8. Suppose that the U.S. and England form a free trade area called USUK, and that total trade between them is 100 in a year when their combined trade with other nations is 100. If total world trade, including all trade for the USUK countries is 1000, then what is the value for the USUK trade concentration ratio?
    a.   1.0
    b.   2.2
    c.   0.50
    d.   2.5
    e.   none of the above

9. What is the name given to the gain to home consumers that no group within the home country loses if the home country enters into a free trade agreement with another country?
    a.   regionalism
    b.   trade diversion
    c.   trade deflection
    d.   trade creation
    e.   none of the above

10. What do we call the loss to a home country that enters into a free trade agreement with a country that is not a low cost producer in any product?
    a.   regionalism
    b.   trade diversion
    c.   trade deflection
    d.   trade creation
    e.   none of the above

11. What general rule should a country follow when entering into free trade agreements?
    a.   Include as many countries as possible in the agreement.
    b.   Try to include countries who are low cost producers in some products.
    c.   Try to include countries that are very similar to your country.
    d.   all of the above
    e.   a and b

12. Sometimes when a home country enters into a free trade agreement with several other countries, firms from nonmember countries move their productive facilities to a member country in order to be able to export into the home country. This is called
    a.   regionalism.
    b.   trade diversion.
    c.   trade deflection.
    d.   trade creation.
    e.   none of the above

13. A "most favored nation" is one with
    a.   whom we have negotiated a free trade agreement.
    b.   a high standard of living.
    c.   a highly skilled labor force.
    d.   large endowments of natural resources.
    e.   none of the above

14. GATT has been promoting
    a.   regionalism.
    b.   trade diversion.
    c.   trade deflection.
    d.   multilateralism.
    e.   none of the above

15. Which one of the following is not a member of NAFTA?
    a.   Canada
    b.   Mexico
    c.   Chile
    d.   U.S.
    e.   all of the above are members

16. Which one of the following is not a member of MERCUSOR?
    a.   Brazil
    b.   Argentina
    c.   Paraguay
    d.   Uruguay
    e.   all of the above are members

17. If the U.S. unilaterally lowers tariffs on many products from poor countries, this is an example of
    a.   a preferential trade arrangement.
    b.   regionalism.
    c.   multilateralism.
    d.   a free trade area.
    e.   none of the above

18. Who sponsored many multilateral trade agreements since WWII?
    a.   WTO
    b.   U.S.
    c.   GATT
    d.   NAFTA
    e.   none of the above

19. If the members of a free trade area trade only with each other, and do not trade at all with anyone else, then the value for their trade concentration ratio is likely to be
    a.   zero.
    b.   +1.
    c.   greater than +1.
    d.   a negative number.
    e.   between zero and +1.

20.   Which provision of a U.S. trade law allows firms to seek protection if imports pose a serious threat to their industry's economic wellbeing?
    a.   section 201
    b.   section 202
    c.   the Reciprocal Trade Agreements Act
    d.   section 102
    e.   none of the above

Short-Answer Questions

1.   Define a free trade area.

2.   Who belongs to NAFTA?

3.   What are the most significant results of NAFTA?

4.   What do we call the loss to a country if it enters into a free trade agreement with a country who is not the low cost producer for any products?

5.   How many countries belong to the European Union?

6.   Section 201 gives U.S. firms the right to petition which U.S. government agency if they feel that imports pose a serious threat to them?

7.   If the WTO finds that a country has not kept a trade agreement, then what does the WTO do?

8.   The European Union illustrates what type of economic integration?

9.   List four degrees of economic integration from the least integrated to the most integrated.

10.   In order to avoid excessive trade deflection, many free trade areas and customs unions impose what type of rules?

CHAPTER SIX

Balance of Payments and Foreign Exchange Markets

Chapter Overview

Chapter 6 covers two broad topics, namely alternative measures of a country's international transactions, and the demand and supply for foreign exchange that interact to determine the exchange rate. The former begins with the definition of the **balance of payments accounting statement** that records all international transactions by the residents of a country over a time interval, usually one year. The balance of payments accounting statement is a **double entry system**, which means that all international transactions require two entries, a credit (or plus) entry and a debit (or minus) entry. As a general rule, when the home country, say the U.S., sells anything internationally, the sale receives a credit or plus entry, while the payment that we receive is a minus or debit entry. Alternatively, if the U.S. buys anything internationally, this creates a debit or minus entry, and our payment for this purchase is a plus or credit entry.

Because of the double entry nature of the balance of payments accounting statement, it follows that theoretically the sum of all credits always equals the sum of all debits. (In practice there are errors and omissions in recording international transactions, but these will be ignored for now.) Economists, however, choose certain subsets of the entries and calculate net values for them. A net positive sum is called a "surplus" and a net negative sum is called a "deficit."

For example, merchandise exports minus merchandise imports equals the **merchandise balance of trade** surplus (if it is positive) or merchandise balance of trade deficit (if it is negative). The **balance of goods, services and income** is given by the merchandise balance of trade plus (exports of services and income earned from investments abroad) minus (imports of services and income earned by foreigners from their investments here).

Net unilateral transfer payments are defined as the value of gifts that the U.S. receives from abroad minus the value of gifts (including foreign aid) that the U.S. gives to foreigners. If the value for net unilateral transfers is added to the balance of goods, services, and income the result is the **balance on current account**. The current account balance is the most frequently used measure of a country's net sales or purchases internationally.

The **capital account balance** (which is often called the **net capital flow**) is calculated by summing the value of purchases of assets from Americans by foreigners (which is called a **capital inflow**) and subtracting from it the value of U.S. purchases of assets from foreigners (which is called a **capital outflow**). These assets include stocks, bonds, houses, land, office buildings, factories, as well as bank loans and deposits. To explain the last item, when a U.S. bank makes a loan to a foreigner, it is viewed as though the bank is buying the IOU of the foreign borrower. Also, if a U.S. resident places funds in a foreign bank, it is viewed as though the U.S. resident is buying the foreign bank's CD or savings passbook, or checking account.

Governments (especially their central banks) typically hold foreign currency and other foreign financial assets. When the governments buy or sell some of these assets, the net value of such activities is referred to as the **official settlements balance**. We know that the double entry nature of the balance of payments accounting statement implies that theoretically (if there were no errors or omissions) the sum of all entries would be zero. In this case, the sum of the current account balance plus the net capital account balance plus the official settlements balance would always be zero. (Note well that this implies that the "official settlements balance" = – [current account + net capital flow]. However, in reality many international transactions are not reported accurately or at all. Consequently, the balance of payments accounting statement includes a **statistical discrepancy** entry that ensures that the overall balance of payments always equals zero.

The other broad topic covered in Chapter 6 deals with alternative measures of the exchange rate, and the demand and supply framework that many economists use to explain how exchange rates are determined. The foreign exchange market is a system of banks, brokers, and central banks wherein one currency is exchanged for another. The **bilateral nominal exchange rate** is the rate at which one country's money exchanges for another, and this can be expressed as, for example, dollars per euro or euros per dollar. If it takes more dollars to buy a euro today than it did in the past, then the euro has **appreciated** and the dollar has **depreciated**, and conversely if dollars per euro decrease.

Typically, but not always, an international purchase of goods, services, or assets requires the buyer to make payment in the currency of the seller. For example, a wine wholesaler in the U.S. might have to pay for imports of French wine with euros. In order to do so, the wholesaler must buy euros with dollars, thereby giving rise to a demand for euros in the foreign exchange market. In a similar manner, any sale of goods, services, or assets by a resident of the EU is likely to generate a demand for euros.

On the other hand, if a German firm buys an IBM computer, then it is likely to need dollars in order to make payment. Thus, the German firm will sell euros and buy dollars, thereby creating a supply of euros in the foreign exchange market. Similar logic leads to the general conclusion that any international purchase of goods, services, or assets by residents of the EU generates a supply of euros in the foreign exchange market.

The interaction of the supply of and the demand for euros in the foreign exchange market leads to an equilibrium exchange rate wherein the quantity supplied equals the quantity demanded for euros. The demand and supply curves for euros will shift if an event (other than an exchange rate variations) induces a change in the quantity of EU international sales (which shifts the demand for euros) or in the quantity of EU international purchases (which shifts the supply of euros).

As in any demand and supply framework, an increase in demand raises the equilibrium price. Within the foreign exchange market, if the demand for euros shifts to the right because an event (other than an exchange rate variation) increases EU international sales of goods, services, or assets, then the euro will appreciate. Shifts to the left in the demand for euros induce a depreciation of the euro. Along the same lines, if an event prompts a shift to the right in the supply of euros (implying that EU international purchases have increased), then the euro will depreciate. A shift to the left for the supply curve for euros will appreciate the euro.

A **real exchange rate** adjusts the nominal exchange rate by multiplying it by the ratio of home to foreign prices. An **effective exchange rate** is a weighted average (expressed in index number form) of many bilateral exchange rates. There are effective **nominal** exchange rates and effective **real** exchange rates. The effective exchange rate measures the overall strength or weakness of a country's currency.

The **spot market** refers to where currencies are exchanged "on the spot" so to speak, even though delivery of large transactions takes two to three days. (However, you can always go to a large bank and buy or sell foreign currency in relatively small amounts and obtain delivery immediately.) The exchange rate in the spot market is called the **spot rate**. The **forward market** refers to where people agree now to buy or sell foreign currency at a specified time in the future at an agreed upon exchange rate that is called the **forward rate.** If the forward rate for the euro exceeds the spot rate for the euro, then there is a **forward premium** for the euro. On the other hand, if the forward euro is cheaper than the spot euro, then there is a **forward discount** on the euro.

The forward market is used to hedge against exchange rate risk. For example, if a U.S. wholesaler of French wine has 60 days in which payment for imports of French wine must be made, then there is a chance that the euro will appreciate in value during the next 60 days. If it does, then the U.S. wholesaler will have to pay more dollars for the wine than would be paid if the wholesaler paid now. In order to avoid this possibility, the U.S. wholesaler can enter into a forward contract today that ensures that euros can be bought in 60 days at an agreed upon exchange rate.

Key Terms and Concepts

Balance of payments accounting statement
Call option
Capital account
Consumer price index
Credit entry
Cross rates
Current account
Currency appreciation
Currency depreciation
Debit entry
Economic exposure
Effective exchange rate
Exchange rate
Forward exchange derivative instruments
Foreign exchange market
Foreign exchange risk
Forward market
Forward premium or discount
Goods
Hedging
Nominal exchange rate
Official settlements balance
Put option
Real exchange rate
Services
Spot market
Transaction exposure
Translation exposure

Multiple-Choice Questions

1. Theoretically, the sum of all the debit and credit entries in the balance of payments accounting statement should equal
    a. +1.
    b. 0.
    c. −1.
    d. minus the current account balance.
    e. none of the above

For questions 2 – 6, use the table below which gives the international transactions for a country during the year 2002.

merchandise exports	200	merchandise imports	400
service imports	100	service exports	300
earnings from investments abroad	50	fgn earnings in home country	100
home sales of assets	500	home purchases of assets	650
home gifts to foreigners	50	fgn gifts to home country	150

2.   What is the value for the home country's merchandise trade balance in the table above?
    a.   +200
    b.   −200
    c.   +400
    d.   −400
    e.   none of the above

3.   What is the value for the home country's balance of goods, services, and income in the table above?
    a.   −50
    b.   +50
    c.   +100
    d.   −100
    e.   none of the above

4.   What is the value for the home country's current account balance in the table above?
    a.   +100
    b.   −100
    c.   +50
    d.   −50
    e.   none of the above

5.   In the table above, what is the value for the capital account balance?
    a.   +100
    b.   −100
    c.   −150
    d.   +150
    e.   none of the above

6.   In the table above, if the statistical discrepancy is zero, then what is the value for the official settlements balance?
    a.   +100
    b.   −100
    c.   +50
    d.   −50
    e.   none of the above

7. What name is given to the weighted average value of many exchange rates for the home country's currency?
   a. the spot rate
   b. the forward rate
   c. the nominal exchange rate
   d. the effective exchange rate
   e. none of the above

8. If the spot euro sells for $1 and the forward euro sells for $1.05, then there is a forward
   a. discount on the euro of 5%.
   b. discount of 105% on the euro.
   c. premium on the euro of 5%.
   d. premium on the euro of roughly 4.7%.
   e. none of the above

9. If the euro sells for $1.10 and the exchange rate between the euro and pound is 2 euros per pound, then what is the cross rate between the dollar and the pound in units of dollars per pound?
   a. $0.55 per pound
   b. $2/1.10 per pound
   c. $2.20 per pound
   d. $3.22 per pound
   e. none of the above

10. If the spot rate was 10 pesos per dollar yesterday, and now it is 11 pesos per dollar, then what has happened to the value of the peso?
    a. It has depreciated.
    b. It has appreciated.
    c. It has not necessarily appreciated or depreciated, because we don't know about prices in Mexico versus the U.S.
    d. It has not changed.

11. If the nominal exchange rate is $1 per euro when the price level in the U.S. is 100 and the price level in the EU is 50, then what is the value for the real exchange rate in units of U.S. goods per unit of EU goods?
    a. 2
    b. 3
    c. 1
    d. 0.5
    e. none of the above

12. If the euro depreciates from $0.90 per euro to $0.85 per euro, then what will happen to the dollar price of U.S. imports from the EU?
    a. They will rise.
    b. They will remain unchanged.
    c. They will fall.
    d. It is totally impossible to determine.

13. What will happen to the euro price of U.S. exports to Europe in the previous question?
    a.   They will rise.
    b.   They will remain unchanged.
    c.   They will fall.
    d.   It is totally impossible to determine.

14. If an American importer of lumber from Canada wants to hedge against an exchange rate loss on its bill of 1 million Canadian dollars worth of logs that must be paid with Canadian dollars in 90 days, then what will the importer do?
    a.   Sell Canadian dollars spot.
    b.   Buy Canadian dollars forward.
    c.   Sell Canadian dollars forward.
    d.   none of the above

15. An American buys a call option for euros. This means that the American
    a.   must buy euros in the future at some specified exchange rate.
    b.   has the right to buy euros in the future at some specified exchange rate.
    c.   must sell euros in the future at some specified exchange rate.
    d.   has the right to sell euros in the future at some specified exchange rate.

16. An American firm has most of its sales to the EU, and it is afraid that the exchange rate might change in a direction that will reduce the dollar value of its sales. This represents an example of
    a.   cross rates of exchange.
    b.   a put option.
    c.   economic exposure.
    d.   translation exposure.
    e.   none of the above

17. An American bank that is located in Ohio does a great deal of business in Mexico. On its balance sheet it has a large number of loans to Mexican firms that will be repaid in pesos. The bank is worried that the peso might depreciate in the near future. What would this do to the bank's assets and net worth as measured in dollars, and what type of exposure is this?
    a.   Its assets and net worth would fall and this is economic exposure.
    b.   Its assets and net worth would rise and this is economic exposure.
    c.   Its assets and net worth would fall and this is transactions exposure.
    d.   Its assets and net worth would fall and this is translation exposure.
    e.   none of the above

18. An American **put** option in the foreign exchange, FX, market gives the owner the right to
    a.   sell FX at any time before the contract expires.
    b   buy FX at any time before the contract expires.
    c.   sell FX at only one date in the future.
    d.   buy FX at only one date in the future.

19. A European **call** option in the foreign exchange, FX, market gives the owner the right to
    a.   sell FX at any time before the contract expires.
    b.   buy FX at any time before the contract expires.
    c.   sell FX at only one date in the future.
    d.   buy FX at only one date in the future.

20. The price at which the holder of a futures option can exercise the right to buy or sell is called the
    a. exercise price.
    b. equilibrium price.
    c. strike price.
    d. a and b
    e. a and c

Short-Answer Questions

1. What is the general nature of the balance of payments accounting statement?

2. What are the general rules with regard to credit (+) and debit (−) entries in the balance of payments accounting statement?

3. If there are no errors or omissions in measuring international transactions, then what will be the value for the overall balance of payments?

4. What are the components of the current account balance?

5. What name do we give a weighted average of many bilateral exchange rates?

6. If the exchange rate goes from $0.96 per euro to $0.89 per euro, then what has happened to the value for the dollar?

7. What is the value for the real exchange rate in units of U.S. goods per EU goods, if the nominal exchange rate is $1 per euro, while the U.S. price index is 150 and the EU price index is 200?

8. What do we call the situation wherein the spot euro is selling for $1 and the forward euro is selling for $0.95?

9. If the facts in #8 are true on a day when people believe that the euro will be worth $1.10 in the near future, then what will speculators do in the forward market?

10. What is the cross rate of exchange in dollars per euro if it takes $1.50 to buy a pound, and a pound sells for 3 euros?

CHAPTER SEVEN

Exchange Rate Systems, Past to Present

Chapter Overview

Chapter 7 carefully explains the details of the alternative exchange rate systems that have existed from the late 1800s until now. This investigation begins with the gold standard, with a careful discussion of its pros and cons. It then moves to an account of the so-called Bretton Woods system that existed from the end of WWII until the early 1970s. Finally, it reviews the flexible exchange rate era of recent decades, as well as the attempts of several countries either to peg their currency to the dollar or to officially adopt the dollar as their legal tender.

From 1837 until 1933 (with the exception of the Civil War years) the dollar was convertible into gold at a fixed price of $20.646 per ounce. This required the government to buy any gold that people wanted to sell or sell any gold that people wanted to buy at this price. In the later 1800s and from 1900 until WWI most of the leading nations of the world also pegged their currency to gold at a fixed price. This meant that there was a fixed exchange rate between all currencies that were tied to gold. For example, if one ounce of gold is worth $35 or seven British pounds, this means that it takes $35 to buy seven pounds, thereby yielding an exchange rate of five dollars per pound. The exchange rate implied by each currency's price for gold was called the **mint parity rate**. One positive aspect of the gold standard was that exchange rates remained fixed for many decades, and it is believed that this stimulated international trade and investments.

Since each currency is backed by gold under the gold standard, governments cannot simply print new money any time that they desire. Thus, under a gold standard the government loses control of the money supply, which means that money increases only when the stock of gold increases. This has the advantage of keeping the monetary growth rate low in general. Hence, the inflation rate remains low in general. However, a disadvantage of the gold standard is that the government cannot stimulate the economy during an economic downswing via rapid increases in the money supply, unless, by chance, new gold was found. Another disadvantage of the gold standard is that the discovery of large deposits of gold (as in the Gold Rush years beginning in 1848 in the U.S.) means that the money supply and price level will increase rapidly.

Every country but the U.S. cut their currency's ties to gold during WWI, but then many of the leading nations returned to the gold standard during the 1920s. The UK made the mistake of choosing a pound price for gold that was too low, because the mint parity exchange rates between the pound and other currencies yielded such a high price for pounds that British goods were uncompetitive in world markets. This decreased UK exports and increased UK imports to such an extent that the British unemployment rate increased significantly, thereby initiating the Great Depression in England. Thus, another possible negative aspect of the gold standard is that a country's economy can be devastated if an incorrect value for gold is chosen.

During the Great Depression, Britain first, then eventually all other nations, discarded the gold standard. Near the end of WWII a series of meetings at Bretton Woods, New Hampshire established a new system of exchange rates that amounted to a **gold-dollar standard** which is usually called the **Bretton Woods** system. The basic idea was that the dollar was pegged to gold at $35 per ounce, and every other currency was pegged either to gold or to the dollar. The latter meant that every other government had to buy dollars with their home currency or sell dollars in order to buy their home currency in unlimited amounts at a fixed price. This established a fixed exchange rate between the dollar and every other currency and, hence, a fixed exchange rate between every pair of currencies. Thus, the dollar served as a **reserve currency** during the Bretton Woods era.

The **International Monetary Fund**, IMF, was established to run the Bretton Woods system. Its main function was to lend dollars or gold to countries who needed them (when they ran out of their reserves of dollars) in order to buy their currency with dollars. During the Bretton Woods system, other governments could buy gold from the U.S. government, but private citizens could not do so. Since all governments needed dollars in order to support the value of their currency (by buying their currency with dollars) they (with the exception of France) did not buy much gold from the U.S.

However, by the 1960s the total amount of dollars held by foreign governments exceeded the value of the U.S. gold stock. This meant that they could not possibly sell all of their dollars to us for gold. This created problems that eventually led to the end of the Bretton Woods system. The end began in August, 1971 when the dollar was temporarily floated and then officially devalued 10% with regard to gold in December 1971. The latter represented an attempt to restore the Bretton Woods system and is referred to as the **Smithsonian Agreement**, but the system eventually failed once and for all in 1973.

At that time, the major currencies, e.g., the dollar, pound, duetsche mark, french franc, swiss franc, yen, and Canadian dollar, floated against each other, which means that the supply and demand for each currency in FX markets determined the exchange rate. In recent years the major European currencies (with exception of the pound) have been replaced by the euro, which floats against the pound, yen, dollar, swiss franc, and Canadian dollar.

A flexible exchange rate system was against the rules that the IMF was supposed to enforce, but at the **Jamaica Accord** in 1976 the IMF gave its blessing to any exchange rate system that each country might choose. Even though the major currencies had flexible exchange rates, the system is called a **dirty float** because governments often engage in FX market intervention, whereby they buy or sell their home currency in an attempt to influence exchange rates.

As an example, the dollar appreciated roughly 50% overall in the first half of the 1980s, and it appeared as though this appreciation might continue. Consequently, the leading industrial nations had a meeting in 1985 and announced the **Plaza Agreement** whereby each government would sell large amounts of dollars in order to reverse the five year appreciation of the dollar. The result was that the dollar depreciated approximately as much in the next two years as it had appreciated in the previous five years. This lead to the **Louvre Accord** in 1987 at which the major countries announced that they would no longer sell dollars, because its value had fallen sufficiently. All of this is one example of the **high volatility** of exchange rates during the flexible exchange rate era.

Even though the major currencies of the world have floated against each other since the early 1970s, many other currencies are pegged to a major currency or pegged to a **currency basket.** For example, Hong Kong and (until 2002) Argentina established a fixed dollar value for the Hong Kong dollar and the Argentine peso. One advantage of this is that a stable exchange rate with respect to the dollar induces foreign firms to build facilities in your country, and it makes it less risky to engage in international trade. However, a major disadvantage of pegging to the dollar is that the value of home money appreciates or depreciates with regard to third currencies as the dollar appreciates or depreciates. Thus, the appreciation of the dollar in the late 1990s and early 2000s meant that the Argentine peso also appreciated, and this made Argentine goods so uncompetitive in world markets that the Argentine economy collapsed.

Finally, some countries have decided to adopt the dollar as the official currency for their country. This was done by Ecuador in 2000 and El Salvador in 20001. The main advantage of **dollarization**, as this is called, is that it means that the value of a country's legal tender (which is now the dollar) is relatively stable in value. No one needs to fear that the government is going to rapidly expand its money supply and create high inflation. One disadvantage is that the prices in world markets of country's products will rise and fall with the value of the dollar in FX markets. Another disadvantage is that dollarized country cannot increase its money supply unless it sells more to the U.S. than it buys.

Alternatively, if the dollarized country buys excessively from the U.S., then dollars will flow out of it, thereby reducing the money within the country and, perhaps, creating macro-economic problems.

Key Terms and Concepts

Bretton Woods system
Convertibility
Crawling band
Crawling peg
Currency basket
Currency board
Dirty float
Dollar-standard exchange-rate system
Dollarization
Exchange-rate band
Exchange-rate system
Flexible exchange-rate system
Group of seven, G7
International monetary fund, IMF
Jamaica accord
Gold standard
Mint parity rate
Monetary order
Overvalued currency
Pegged exchange-rate system
Plaza agreement
Reserve currency
Revalue
Smithsonian agreement
Undervalued currency
World Bank

Multiple-Choice Questions

1. The gold standard ended once and for all
    a. in 1900.
    b. during WWI.
    c. during the Great Depression.
    d. during WWII.
    e. in the early 1970s.

2. If an ounce of gold is worth $50 or 20 pounds sterling, then what is the mint parity exchange rate in dollars per pound?
    a. $2.50
    b. $0.40
    c. $100
    d. $0.25
    e. none of the above

3. If the dollar price of gold in #2 changes to $60 per ounce, but one ounce is still worth 20 pounds sterling, then what has happened to the dollar's value with regard to gold, what is the new dollars per pound exchange rate, and what has happened to the value for the pound?
   a. The $ revalued, the exchange rate is $3/pound, and the pound has depreciated.
   b. The $ devalued, the exchange rate is $0.33/pound, and the pound depreciated.
   c. The $ devalued, the exchange rate is $3/pound, and the pound appreciated.
   d. The $ revalued, the exchange rate is $3/pound, and the pound appreciated.
   e. none of the above

4. When a country is on a gold standard then
   a. the government must buy or sell gold at a fixed price.
   b. the government loses control of its money supply.
   c. exchange rates are fixed if other countries are also on the gold standard.
   d. all of the above
   e. none of the above

5. During the Bretton Woods system
   a. the price of gold was fixed at $35 per ounce.
   b. other currencies were pegged to gold or to the dollar.
   c. countries had to get IMF approval for exchange rate variations exceeding 5%.
   d. all of the above
   e. none of the above

6. The World Bank
   a. is another name for the IMF.
   b. makes long term loans for economic development.
   c. makes loans to countries with exchange rate and/or financial problems.
   d. all of the above
   e. none of the above

7. Which of the following was an attempt to re-establish the Bretton Woods system?
   a. the Smithsonian Agreement
   b. the Jamaica Accord
   c. the Plaza Agreement
   d. the Louvre Accord
   e. none of the above

8. Which of the following gave each country the right to decide on its exchange rate system?
   a. the Smithsonian Agreement
   b. the Jamaica Accord
   c. the Plaza Agreement
   d. the Louvre Accord
   e. none of the above

9. Which of the following was an announcement that the dollar had fallen in value sufficiently, and, thus, governments were no longer going to sell dollars consistently?
    a.   the Smithsonian Agreement
    b.   the Jamaica Accord
    c.   the Plaza Agreement
    d.   the Louvre Accord
    e.   none of the above

10. Which of the following was an announcement that the dollar had appreciated excessively and that governments were going to sell dollars?
    a.   the Smithsonian Agreement
    b.   the Jamaica Accord
    c.   the Plaza Agreement
    d.   the Louvre Accord
    e.   none of the above

11. If the dollar is pegged to gold at $35 per ounce, and the yen is pegged to the dollar at 200 yen per dollar, while the UK pound is pegged at $5 per pound, then what is the exchange rate in yen per pound?
    a.   40 yen per pound
    b.   1000 yen per pound
    c.   25 yen per pound
    d.   1/40 yen per pound
    e.   none of the above

12. Currently, what is a function of the IMF?
    a.   Making long term loans for economic development.
    b.   Approving of exchange rate variations.
    c.   Making loans to countries with exchange rate and/or financial problems.
    d.   all of the above
    e.   none of the above

13. When did the Bretton Woods system end?
    a.   during WWI
    b.   during the Great Depression
    c.   during WWII
    d.   in the early 1970s
    e.   none of the above

14. A "dirty float" refers to when
    a.   exchange rates can always float freely.
    b.   governments intervene to influence flexible exchange rates.
    c.   drug money is used to buy dollars.
    d.   a currency board replaces a central bank.
    e.   none of the above

15. The "revaluation" of a currency means that it takes
    a. less of the currency to buy an ounce of gold.
    b. more of the currency to buy an ounce of gold.
    c. more of the currency to buy another currency.
    d. none of the above

16. A currency board
    a. replaces a central bank.
    b. holds reserves of a leading currency, such as dollars.
    c. maintains a fixed exchange rate for its currency with regard to a leading currency.
    d. all of the above
    e. none of the above

17. Dollarization means that a country
    a. replaces its currency with dollars.
    b. pegs its currency to the dollar.
    c. has a currency board that uses dollars as reserves.
    d. all of the above
    e. none of the above

18. What happened to the exchange rate value for the dollar during the first half of the 1980s?
    a. It fell roughly 50%.
    b. It increased more than 100%.
    c. It stayed remarkably constant.
    d. Iit fluctuated mildly with no net change in value.
    e. none of the above

19. What happened to the exchange rate value for the dollar from 1985 to 1987?
    a. It fell sharply.
    b. It increased roughly 50%.
    c. It stayed remarkably constant.
    d. It fluctuated mildly with no net change in value.
    e. none of the above

20. The flexible exchange rate era since the early 1970s has
    a. had surprisingly stable exchange rates.
    b. shown a steady depreciation of the dollar.
    c. experienced exchange rates that are highly volatile.
    d. shown a steady appreciation of the dollar.
    e. none of the above

Short–Answer Questions

1. What is true about exchange rates when all countries are on the gold standard?

2. What does the World Bank do?

3.   What happens to a country's money supply if it is on the gold standard and there is a major discovery of gold deposits?

4.   What happens to a country's money supply if it is on the gold standard and it becomes unprofitable to mine and refine gold?

5.   What was the price of gold during the Bretton Woods system?

6.   When did the Bretton Woods system end?

7.   What has been the most important characteristic of the flexible exchange rate era?

8.   What is the primary function of the IMF today?

9.   What was the Plaza Agreement?

10.   Which are better, fixed exchange rates or flexible exchange rates?

CHAPTER EIGHT

The Power of Arbitrage – Purchasing Power and Interest Rate Parities

Chapter Overview

Chapter 8 carefully investigates two fundamental concepts that are tied up with the idea that market forces should keep the average price level (adjusted for the exchange rate) in all countries about the same, and should keep the rates of return on similar assets approximately equal. The equality of prices is referred to as **purchasing power parity**, PPP, while the equality of rates of return is called **interest parity**. There are two versions of PPP, namely **absolute PPP** and **relative PPP**. Furthermore, there are three versions of interest parity, **covered interest parity**, CIP, **uncovered interest parity**, UIP, and **real interest parity**, RIP. One reason that economists and practitioners are interested in these topics is that each of them has implications with regard to what value the exchange rate either should be or will be in the future.

Absolute purchasing power parity, PPP, requires the average price level at home, P, to equal the price level in any foreign country, P*, multiplied by the spot rate of exchange, S, in units of home money needed to buy one unit of foreign money. That is, absolute PPP holds when P = SP*. The right side of this equation gives the home currency price of foreign goods and services. For example, if the U.S. is the home country and the EU is the foreign country, then the spot exchange rate indicates $ per euro, and SP* measures the amount of dollars needed to buy a representative basket of EU goods and services. If this equals the amount of dollars needed to purchase a representative basket of U.S. goods and services, P, then a dollar has equal purchasing power if it is spent in the U.S. or in the EU. The absolute PPP equation can be solved for the exchange rate as S = P/P*, which is called the PPP value for the spot rate.

An alternative way to view absolute PPP is to recall that the definition of the real exchange rate is SP*/P. Hence, if absolute PPP holds, then the real exchange rate equals plus unity. Many scholarly studies show that the real exchange rate is rarely equal to +1; thus, absolute PPP almost never holds precisely. However, when the real exchange rate moves away from +1, there appears to be a tendency for the real exchange rate to move back toward +1 in the very long run, say over several decades. This implies that there is a tendency for the nominal exchange rate to always revert back toward its PPP value, even though it usually diverges from its PPP value. The convergence toward PPP is very slow, with a half-life of three to seven years. .

Relative PPP is based upon the idea that at any point in time, the real exchange rate might be constant, even though it does not equal +1. In this case, the relative PPP equation becomes: (%? P) = (%? S) + (%? P*). The term on the left side of this equation is the home, say U.S., inflation rate, while the (%? P*) on the right side is the foreign, say EU, inflation rate. If this equation is solved for the (%? S) we see that relative PPP implies that the spot rate will increase (i.e., the euro will appreciate, and the dollar will depreciate) if the inflation rate in the U.S. exceeds the inflation rate in the EU. There is much evidence that over long periods of time, the currency of a high inflation country tends to depreciate, which implies that relative PPP is useful guide for predicting movements in the exchange rate over long time intervals, i.e., at least five to ten years. However, scholarly studies show that relative PPP rarely holds over relatively brief time intervals.

Covered interest parity, CIP, holds if the rate of return on an interest earning asset (such as bonds) at home, R, approximately equals the rate of return on a similar asset abroad after the investor has used the forward market to hedge against any exchange rate loss. To explain, if an American investor buys English government bonds that pay an interest rate of R*, the investor might lose if the pound depreciates in the near future. To avoid this, the American investor can buy pounds spot (in order to pay for the British bonds) at the current spot rate, S, and simultaneously sell pounds forward at the current value for the forward rate, F.

If F and S are equal, then the rate of return for an American investor placing funds in England is simply the interest rate on British bonds, R*. However, if the forward rate exceeds the spot rate, then a profit will be earned when pounds are bought spot and sold forward. For example, if the spot pound sells for $1, but the forward pound sells for $1.02, then the 2% profit equals the forward premium on the pound, (F-S)/S. This must be added to R* to obtain the total rate of return for an American investor who places covered funds in England. Hence, CIP holds if R = R* + (F-S)/S. There is much evidence that suggests that CIP almost always holds.

If, on the other hand, an American investor places funds in England but does not use the forward market to hedge against an exchange rate loss, then the expected rate of return on this investment equals the English interest rate, R*, plus the expected future percentage change in the value for the pound, %? S^e. For example if R* = 0.05, and the investor expects the pound to go up in value by 3% in the future, then the investor expects to obtain a return of 0.05 + 0.03 = 0.08 by placing uncovered funds in England. If this equals the rate of return on funds invested in the U.S., R, then uncovered interest parity, UIP, holds. Thus, the UIP condition is: R = R* + %? S^e.

Notice that the UIP equation can be solved for %? S^e = R – R*, suggests that future changes in the spot rate will depend on the interest rate differential. Unfortunately, scores of scholarly studies suggest that UIP does not hold, even when account is taken of the fact that one asset might be more risky than another so that a risk premium has to be added to the UIP equation.

Market efficiency is defined broadly to mean that the return on or price of a financial asset should reflect all available information. Efficiency implies that similar assets should have the same returns, which, in turn, means that both CIP and UIP will hold if the FX market is efficient. However, an examination of the CIP and UIP equations, implies that when they hold simultaneously, then the forward premium or discount should equal the expected percentage change in the spot rate. If exchange rate expectations are not consistently wrong in the same direction, then we say that expectations are rational, or equivalently that rational expectations, RE, exist. In this case, exchange rate expectations are, on average, correct, even though they might usually be a little too high or too low. Thus, if the FX market is efficient and if RE exist, then the forward premium or discount should predict what happens to the spot rate in the future. However, scores of scholarly studies indicate that this is not true.

The interest rates used in the CIP and UIP equations are nominal interest rates. The real interest rate in the U.S. equals the nominal rate, R, minus the expected inflation rate in the U.S., %? P^e. Similarly, the real rate of interest abroad equals R* – % ? P^{e*}. If international financial markets are highly integrated (which means that funds can always flow freely to where they can earn the highest return), then real interest parity, RIP, will hold, i.e., R – % ? P^e = R* – % ? P^{e*}. Empirical studies suggest that RIP rarely holds in a precise manner, but differences from RIP are not large among the most affluent economies.

Key Terms and Concepts

Absolute PPP
Adaptive expectations
Arbitrage
Big Mac index
Covered interest arbitrage
Covered interest parity
Efficient markets hypothesis

Foreign exchange market efficiency
Law of one price
Purchasing power parity, PPP
Rational expectations
Real interest parity
Real interest rate
Relative PPP
Risk premium
Uncovered interest arbitrage
Uncovered interest parity

Multiple-Choice Questions

1. Which of the following refers to the fact that any given **one** product should sell for the same price regardless of where it is produced and sold?
    a. law of one price
    b. absolute PPP
    c. relative PPP
    d. CIP
    e. none of the above

2. Arbitrage refers to
    a. buying high and selling cheap.
    b. buying cheap and selling high.
    c. diversifying an investment portfolio internationally.
    d. all of the above
    e. none of the above

3. If the U.S. price index, P, is 100 when the EU price index, P*, is 50 when the spot rate, S, is $1.50 per euro, then what is the value for the real exchange rate in units of U.S. goods per EU goods?
    a. 0.67
    b. 0.33
    c. 0.75
    d. 0.50
    e. none of the above

4. What is true in #3?
    a. Absolute PPP does not hold.
    b. The euro is undervalued.
    c. The dollar is overvalued.
    d. all of the above
    e. none of the above

5. What is the PPP value for the spot rate in #3?
    a. $0.50 per euro
    b. $0.75 per euro
    c. $2.00 per euro
    d. $1.50 per euro
    e. none of the above

6.   If relative PPP holds, then the real exchange rate
      a.   always equals +1.
      b.   is constant.
      c.   always equals zero.
      d.   none of the above

7.   What happens to the value for the pound if relative PPP holds in a year when the U.S. inflation rate
      is 3% and the inflation rate in England is 5%?
      a.   The pound appreciates 2%.
      b.   The pound depreciates 2%.
      c.   The pound appreciates 8%.
      d.   The pound depreciates 8%.
      e.   none of the above

8.   Why might absolute PPP not hold?
      a.   Transportation costs between countries might be high.
      b.   Tariffs or quotas exist.
      c.   The home basket of goods might differ from the foreign basket of goods.
      d.   all of the above
      e.   none of the above

9.   The Big Mac Index refers to using the
      a.   prices of Big Macs in different countries to calculate the PPP value for the spot rate.
      b.   index of sales of Big Macs in different countries to determine where the Big Mac is cheapest.
      c.   prices of Big Macs in different countries to determine where McDonalds faces the strongest
            competition.
      d.   home runs hit by Mark McGuire at each date in the season to see if a current baseball player
            is on pace to hit more than 60 home runs.
      e.   none of the above

10.   Suppose that the U.S. interest rate is 6% when the interest rate in Japan is 2%, the spot rate is $1 per
      yen, and the forward rate is $1.02 per yen. Is there a forward premium or a forward discount for the
      yen, and what is its value?
      a.   A forward premium for the yen equals 2%.
      b.   A forward discount for the yen equals 2%.
      c.   A forward premium for the yen equals 4%.
      d.   A forward discount for the yen equals 4%.
      e.   none of the above

11.   What is the covered rate of return for an American investor who places covered funds in Japan in
      #10?
      a.   +2%
      b.   −2%
      c.   −4%
      d.   +4%
      e.   none of the above

12. Does CIP hold in #10? If not, then which way will funds move?
    a. Yes, CIP holds.
    b. No, CIP does not hold and funds will move to Japan.
    c. No, CIP does not hold and funds will move to the U.S.
    d. It is impossible to determine with the given information.

13. Which of the following is true?
    a. UIP almost always holds.
    b. CIP almost always holds.
    c. Absolute PPP almost always holds.
    d. all of the above
    e. none of the above

14. Assume that the U.S. interest rate is 4% when the interest rate in the EU is 7%. Also, let the spot rate be $1 per euro, and the expected future spot rate is $0.96 per euro. What is the expected uncovered rate of return for a U.S. investor who places funds in the EU?
    a. 7%
    b. 5%
    c. 11%
    d. 4%
    e. none of the above

15. Does UIP hold in #14? If not, then which way will funds move?
    a. Yes, UIP holds.
    b. No, and funds move to the U.S.
    c. No, and funds move to the EU.
    d. It is impossible to determine with the given information.

16. Adaptive expectations with regard to the exchange rate mean that people use
    a. all available information to determine their expectations.
    b. all available information and the latest theories to determine their expectations.
    c. only past data on the exchange rate to determine their expectations.
    d. none of the above

17. Foreign exchange market efficiency and rational expectations together imply that
    a. the forward rate will be a good predictor of the future spot rate.
    b. relative PPP holds.
    c. absolute PPP holds.
    d. a risk premium exists.
    e. none of the above

18. What is the inflation rate in England if real interest parity, RIP, holds when the U.S. inflation rate is 4%, and interest rates are 9% in the U.S. and 6% in England?
    a. 2%
    b. 3%
    c. 4%
    d. 1%
    e. none of the above

19.   Assume that risk-adjusted UIP holds between U.S. and Mexican government bonds, even though Mexican bonds are considered to be more risky, i.e., a nonzero risk premium, RP, exists. If the U.S. interest rate is 5% while the Mexican interest rate is 18% in a year when people expect the peso to depreciate by 10%, then what is the value for the risk premium?
       a.   +0.03
       b.   −0.03
       c.   +0.23
       d.   −0.23
       e.   none of the above

20.   U.S. and Japanese government bonds are considered to be equally risky. UIP holds when the U.S. interest rate is 5% and the Japanese interest rate is 2%. If the current spot rate is $1 per yen, then what is the value for the expected future spot rate in $ per yen?
       a. $1.01 per yen
       b. $1.02 per yen
       c. $1.03 per yen
       d. $0.97 per yen
       e.   none of the above

Short-Answer Questions

1.   What is the absolute PPP condition algebraically, and what does this mean?

2.   If $P < SP^*$, then is home money overvalued or undervalued?

3.   If UIP holds when the U.S. interest rate is 8% and the English interest rate is 4%, then what do people expect the pound to do in the future?

4.   What does empirical evidence suggest with regard to movements in the real exchange rate back toward +1 during those periods when the real exchange rate differs significantly from +1?

5.   If a portfolio manager for an insurance company is not permitted to take any exchange rate risks, then what two FX market transactions will the manager engage in if it is profitable to place funds in an EU bank?

6.   If FX market efficiency holds and if exchange rate expectations are rational when people expect the euro to appreciate 4% in the next year, then what is the value for the forward discount or forward premium on euros?

7.   Relative PPP predicts what with regard to the exchange rate value of the Mexican peso (in $ per peso) if Mexico typically has a much higher inflation rate than in the U.S.?

8.   If real interest parity holds when the U.S. real rate of interest is 3% and the nominal interest rate in Mexico is 15%, then what is the expected inflation rate in Mexico?

9.   If the pound typically appreciates for six weeks in a row, and then depreciates for the next six weeks, etc., then what would adaptive expectations suggest is going to happen to the pound next week if the pound has changed steadily in value from $1.49 to $1.55 in the last 4 weeks?

10.   Answer #9 if the pound has changed steadily in value from $1.49 to $1.59 over the last 6 weeks.

CHAPTER NINE

Global Money and Banking

Chapter Overview

Chapter 9 examines the monetary aspects of the world economy by reviewing the activities of **central banks** including the instruments of monetary policy, alternative measures of the money supply, how interest rates are, in general, determined, and how attempts by central banks to alter the exchange rate can affect a country's money supply. It also examines how monetary policy is used to influence domestic prices and output.

A central bank (e.g., the Federal Reserve in the U.S., the ECB, European Central Bank, in the EU, and the Bank of England) is an agency of the government that performs several functions. At a perfunctory level it facilitates the **clearing of checks** within the banking system, and it **regulates** the activities of banks. They also function as the **bank for their government**. For example, the treasury department in the U.S. has, in effect, a checking account with the Fed. Furthermore, a central bank serves as a **lender of last resort** for private banks, and it attempts to control or at least **influence the values for the exchange rate, money supply, and/or interest rates** via **monetary policy.**

The **asset side** of the balance sheet of a central bank includes **domestic** assets and **international** assets, which are often called **international reserves**. Domestic assets are **government bonds** and **domestic credit**. The latter is loans to the private sector. In the U.S. the Fed can make loans only to private banks, but some central banks are permitted to lend funds to private businesses. International assets include **gold** and **foreign exchange**, FX. The sum of all central bank assets equals the country's **monetary base**.

The **liabilities** side of the central bank balance sheet includes all **currency** outstanding (i.e., outside of banks) and total **bank reserves** deposited with the central bank. Since central banks tend to have a trivial net worth (in the U.S. the Fed gives all profits back to the U.S. Treasury), it follows that the sum of all liabilities is approximately equal to the sum of all assets. Thus, the monetary base can be viewed as either the sum of all assets, as stated above, or the sum of all central bank liabilities.

The central bank can alter the country's money supply by changing the monetary base, and this can be accomplished via **open market operations** (i.e., buying or selling government bonds) or via **changes in domestic credit**. Also, the money supply can be changed (for any given value for the monetary base) if the central bank alters the **required reserve ratio**, i.e., the percentage of deposits within banks that the banks must keep on reserve. To increase the money supply the central bank can buy government bonds, lend more to domestic banks and firms, and/or decrease the required reserve ratio. The opposite actions will reduce the money supply.

There are several measures of the money supply. The two most important are **M1** which includes: currency plus coins, all transactions or checkable deposits, and travelers' checks, and **M2** which includes everything in M1 plus several items of which the most important are savings account and small time deposit balances. The equilibrium short term interest rate is determined when the **supply** of money equals the **demand** for money. Consequently, if the central bank wishes to reduce short term interest rates, then it will increase the money supply, and vice-versa if it wishes to increase short term interest rates. Typically, long term interest rates quickly vary in the same direction as short term interest rates, but they change less.

Central banks often attempt to alter the exchange rate value for their home currency by buying or selling it in the FX market. This is called **FX market intervention**. They buy their currency with FX in order to put upward pressure on the value of their currency. This purchase is paid for with the FX that is part of the international reserve component of the monetary base. Consequently, efforts to support the exchange rate value of home money tend to reduce both the monetary base and the money supply unless the central bank does something to prevent this. If FX market intervention is allowed to reduce base money and the money supply, it is referred to as **nonsterilized FX market intervention.**

The appropriate action to prevent FX market intervention from altering base money and the money supply is for the central bank either to simultaneously buy government bonds or increase domestic credit when it purchases its currency with FX. These activities raise the domestic asset component of base money and offset the decrease in base money from the loss of FX. Such activities are called **sterilized FX market intervention**.

Scholarly studies suggest that nonsterilized FX market intervention can influence the exchange rate primarily because the simultaneous change in the money supply alters interest rates. However, studies indicate that sterilized intervention has only a very brief affect on the exchange rate, unless it creates an **announcement effect**. The latter occurs if FX market intervention induces private FX market traders to act in a manner that moves the exchange rate in the direction desired by the central bank.

The intersection of an economy's **aggregate demand** and **aggregate supply** curves determine the overall price level, which is called the **GDP deflator**, and total level of output, or **GDP**. Central banks often attempt to alter the price level or output by using monetary policy to shift the aggregate demand curve. For example, if the economy is experiencing an economic downswing, the central bank can increase the money supply via the use of one or more of the three tools at its disposal. The larger money supply means that the money demand and money supply curves will intersect at a lower interest rate. When interest rates are lower, households are more willing to borrow and spend, especially on cars and houses, and firms are more willing to borrow and spend on investment projects. Thus, the expansionary monetary policy shifts the aggregate demand curve to the right and increases the equilibrium level of GDP. The opposite actions by the central bank tend to decrease aggregate demand, which is the appropriate event when the central bank wishes to fight inflation

Key Terms and Concepts

Aggregate demand
Aggregate supply
Announcement effect
Balance sheet
Base year
Central banks
Domestic assets
Domestic credit
Discount rate
Fiscal agent
Foreign exchange market intervention
Gross domestic product, GDP
GDP deflator
Leaning against the wind
Leaning with the wind
Lender of last resort
Lombard rate
M1
M2
Monetary aggregate

Monetary base
Monetary policy
Nominal income
Open market operations
Portfolio balance effect
Real income
Reserve requirements
Sterilization

Multiple-Choice Questions

1. Which of the following is **not** a function of a central bank?
    a. facilitate the clearing of checks
    b. regulate banks
    c. lender of last resort
    d. a fiscal agent for the government
    e. all of the above are functions

2. Which of the following is **not** an asset for a central bank?
    a. government bonds
    b. loans to the private sector
    c. currency outstanding
    d. gold
    e. all of the above are assets

3. Which of the following is **not** a liability for a central bank?
    a. government bonds
    b. currency outstanding
    c. bank reserves
    d. gold
    e. a and d

4. What is the value for the monetary base if the following appear in the central bank's balance sheet? gold = 50; currency outstanding = 100; government bonds = 200; domestic credit = 50; foreign exchange = 50; bank reserves = ?
    a. 350
    b. 300
    c. 250
    d. 450
    e. none of the above

5. What is the value for bank reserves in #4?
    a. 350
    b. 300
    c. 250
    d. 50
    e. none of the above

6.   Which of the following actions by a central bank will **decrease** the money supply?
        a.   raise the required reserve ratio
        b.   sell government bonds
        c.   extend less domestic credit
        d.   all of the above
        e.   none of the above

7.   Which of the following actions by a central bank are appropriate if the bank wants to increase aggregate demand?
        a.   sell government bonds
        b.   buy government bonds
        c.   raise the required reserve ratio
        d.   all of the above
        e.   none of the above

8.   Which interest rate is the one set by the ECB (on loans to banks) above current market interest rates?
        a.   the discount rate
        b.   LIBOR
        c.   the Lombard rate
        d.   marginal interest rate
        e.   c and d

9.   What is the value for the money multiplier if all banks are required to have reserves equal to 10% of the deposits in them?
        a.   10
        b.   2
        c.   5
        d.   100
        e.   none of the above

10.   If the required reserve ratio is 20% when the central bank sells $100 of government bonds, then what will be the ultimate change in deposits at banks?
        a.   +50
        b.   −500
        c.   +500
        d.   +2000
        e.   none of the above

11.   Which of the following is **not** included in the M1 measure of the money supply?
        a.   travelers' checks
        b.   coins
        c.   currency
        d.   transactions or checkable deposits
        e.   All of the above are included in M1.

12. Which of the following is included in the M2 measure of the money supply?
    a.   currency
    b.   transactions or checkable deposits
    c.   savings accounts
    d.   small time deposits
    e.   All of the above are included in M2.

13. What is the value for M1 if the following data exist? (Assume that any items that do not appear here are zero in value.)

small time deposits	200
coins & currency	100
travelers' checks	50
savings accounts	400
transactions or checkable deposits	500

    a.   400
    b.   700
    c.   550
    d.   650
    e.   none of the above

14. What is the value for M2 in the previous question?
    a.   700
    b.   550
    c.   1250
    d.   1050
    e.   none of the above

15. Use the money supply and money demand graph to determine what happens to the equilibrium interest rate if the central bank raises the required reserve ratio for banks. In this case the equilibrium interest rate
    a.   rises.
    b.   falls.
    c.   remains unchanged.
    d.   could rise or fall.

16. How will the central bank's actions in #15 affect the aggregate demand curve and the price level in the economy?
    a.   Aggregate demand decreases and the price level rises.
    b.   Aggregate demand decreases and the price level falls.
    c.   Aggregate demand increases and the price level rises.
    d.   Aggregate demand increases and the price level falls.

17. What happens to the equilibrium interest rate if the central bank buys government bonds? (Use the money supply and money demand graph to determine your answer.)
    a.   It falls.
    b.   It rises.
    c.   It remains unchanged.
    d.   It could rise or fall.

18. What happens to the aggregate demand curve and the equilibrium value for GDP in the previous question?
    a.   Aggregate demand decreases and GDP rises.
    b.   Aggregate demand decreases and GDP falls.
    c.   Aggregate demand increases and GDP rises.
    d.   Aggregate demand increases and GDP falls.

19. What happens to the monetary base, B, the money supply, M, and interest rates, i, if the central bank buys its currency with FX?
    a.   They all rise.
    b.   They all fall.
    c.   B and M rise, while i falls.
    d.   B and M fall, while i rises.
    e.   none of the above

20. What happens to the monetary base, B, the money supply, M, and the interest rate, i, if the central bank sells its currency for FX, and if the central bank engages in an appropriate sterilization activity?
    a.   They all rise
    b.   They all fall
    c.   They are all unchanged.
    d.   B and M rise, and i falls.
    e.   none of the above

Short-Answer Questions

1. What name is given to attempts by a central bank to influence interest rates, or the price level, or the level of GDP?

2. The monetary base is the sum of what items in the central bank's balance sheet?

3. What function of a central bank is tied up with the fact that it always stands ready to lend funds to banks during a financial crisis?

4. What name is given to the narrowest measure of the money supply?

5. What type of open market operation is appropriate if a central bank wants to fight inflation?

6. What is an appropriate sterilization activity when the central bank sells its currency for FX?

7. What happens to the equilibrium interest rate if a central bank engages in unsterilized purchases of its currency in the FX market? Why?

8. What name is given to the weighted average of the prices of all goods and services produced by an economy?

9. What will happen to the overall price level and output if the central bank increases the value for domestic credit? Why?

10. What type of unsterilized FX market intervention is appropriate if home money has been depreciating lately and the central bank wants to lean against the wind?

CHAPTER TEN

Can Globalization Lift All Boats?

Chapter Overview

Chapter 10 deals primarily with the effects of international trade on the distribution of income, both within any given country and between the advanced and developing countries. In the process it reviews the concepts of labor demand and labor market equilibrium. These are used to explain how trade affects wage rates and the level of employment. The chapter explores the increasing importance of world trade and capital flows for developing nations. There are many interesting facts associated with all of these topics.

International trade has steadily become more important for developing countries. The percent of world trade that the developing nations account for increased from 10% in 1980 to roughly 33% in the year 2000. However, the five leading trading partners for the U.S. are predominantly advanced countries. In decreasing order of importance these five countries are: Canada, Mexico, Japan, the United Kingdom, and Germany.

A major complaint within the U.S. about international trade is that it reduces wage rates and employment. Those who believe that this is true point out that from the early 1970s to 2000 the inflation adjusted yearly compensation of male workers among the top 10% of all income groups increased 10%, but for the male workers in the bottom 10% of all income earners the inflation adjusted yearly compensation decreased 20%.

Economists have reasoned that if international trade reduces wage rates in the U.S., then it should have increased wage rates within the economies of our trading partners. There is some evidence that this is, indeed, true. In 1960 the average wage rate in manufacturing for all U.S. trading partners was only 38% of a similar average within the U.S. However, this average wage within our trading partners had risen to 83% of the U.S. wage by the year 2000.

Most countries still have lower labor costs in manufacturing than in the U.S. However, in 1995, Germany, Japan, and Canada all had higher labor costs than in the U.S., with German labor costs being more than 75% higher than in the U.S. By the year 2000 the labor costs in Japan and Canada had dropped slightly below costs in the U.S., because the dollar appreciated between 1995 and 2000 so that the wage rates in yen or Canadian dollars translated into fewer dollars.

The maximum wage that a firm will pay depends on how much revenue a unit of labor generates. The latter is called the **marginal revenue product, MRP,** of labor, and it is calculated by multiplying the **marginal product** of labor by the **marginal revenue** from selling each extra unit of output. In a highly competitive market, the marginal revenue equals the selling price of the product. The MRP of labor curve for each firm is that firm's labor demand curve.

This implies that the total market demand for labor increases or decreases as the MRP of labor varies. In particular, the market demand for labor decreases as the product price decreases. Consequently, the equilibrium **market wage rate** (which is found at the intersection of the market supply of labor curve and the market demand for labor curve) decreases when the product price falls. This also reduces the equilibrium quantity of labor hired.

All of this helps to explain how increased foreign competition can affect wage rates and employment within the U.S. If there are more foreign firms producing the same product as in the U.S., then the world price of this product will fall, thereby reducing the demand for labor within the U.S. This will yield a lower equilibrium market wage rate and, also, decrease the quantity of labor hired.

Furthermore, if Americans import more of any product, this will force U.S. firms to reduce their price in order to remain competitive. The lower product price again reduces wage rates and employment within the U.S.

The factor proportions theory of comparative advantage suggests that wage rates will rise for the type of labor used intensively in a country's export industries. In the U.S. the export industries use relatively much skilled labor. Also, the factor proportions theory suggests that wage rates will fall for the type of labor used intensively in the import competing industries. In the U.S. these industries use relatively much unskilled labor.

The data on wage rates within the U.S. are consistent with these conclusions. In 1950 (when international trade was of much less importance for the U.S.) the average wage for college graduates was 1.4 times the average wage for high school graduates. However, in 2000 (when international trade had grown substantially) a college graduate earned 1.8 times as much as a high school graduate. Even though these changes are consistent with the hypothesis that international trade has caused unskilled workers to have relatively lower wage rates in the U.S., economists believe that there is another (perhaps more important) reason for this fact. Since 1950 the level of technology within our economy has advanced tremendously, and this has increased the demand for skilled workers relative to the demand for unskilled workers. Therefore, the relative wage for unskilled workers would have fallen independently of international trade.

The factor proportions theory of comparative advantage also suggests that wage rates, in general, will rise in countries whose comparative advantage lies in labor intensive products. Since developing nations have a relative abundance of labor (compared to capital), this implies that international trade will increase wage rates in such countries. However, the factor proportions theory also implies that returns to capital in the developing countries will fall.

There is some scholarly evidence that international trade exerts a positive effect on economic growth. In general, countries with fewer barriers to trade have a higher average annual growth rate of income per capita. The reason or reasons for this are not known for certain, but the competition that goes with international trade might induce domestic firms to continuously increase efficiency and to adopt newer more advanced forms of technology. Both events will increase the rate of economic growth.

Economic growth depends in part on the accumulation of capital goods. In a closed economy this requires domestic residents to save and invest. Unfortunately, many developing countries are too poor to save much. However, a developing country can grow by borrowing internationally and/or by attracting foreign firms into their country, i.e., **foreign direct investment**. Even though these two ways of accumulating capital goods are effective, one drawback is that interest on loans and profits earned by foreign firms within a developing country must be paid.

In recent decades capital flows into developing countries have increased very much. In the early and mid-1990s a large percentage of these funds was in the form of shorter-term capital flows, such as deposits into developing country banks and the purchase of short term securities. The flow of short-term capital has proven to be highly volatile. In 1994 in Mexico, and then in 1997-98 in Asian countries, and 1999 in Russia, foreign investors withdrew massive amounts of funds from these countries. This caused their exchange rates to depreciate significantly, and led, in general, to severe economic problems within these developing countries. The flow of funds for foreign direct investment has been much less volatile, and, hence, is a better way for developing countries to accumulate capital.

Key Terms and Concepts

Capital flows
Derived demand for labor
Distribution of income
Economic development

Factor proportions theory
Foreign direct investment
International trade and wages
Inter-industry trade
Intra-industry trade
Law of diminishing marginal returns
Market wage rate
Marginal product of capital
Marginal product of labor
Marginal revenue
Marginal revenue product of capital
Marginal revenue product of labor
Openness
Trade barriers and economic growth

Multiple-Choice Questions

1. What happened between 1980 and 2000 to the percent of world trade associated with developing nations?
   a. It increased from10% to over 50%.
   b. It increased from 25% to 33%.
   c. It increased from 10% to 33%.
   d. It decreased slightly.
   e. none of the above

2. What happened in the U.S. from the early 1970s until 2000 to the compensation of the poorest 10% of male workers?
   a. It increased only 5%.
   b. It decreased about 5%.
   c. It increased 20%.
   d. It decreased 20%.
   e. none of the above

3. What is a major complaint in the U.S. about international trade?
   a. It is not large enough.
   b. It causes inflation.
   c. It lowers wages.
   d. It reduces the number of jobs.
   e. c and d

4. What happened since 1960 to the average wage rate in manufacturing for all of the trading partners for the U.S. compared to the average manufacturing wage in the U.S.?
   a. It increased from 38% to 83%.
   b. It decreased from 83% to 38%.
   c. It stayed about the same.
   d. It increased from 78% to over 100%.
   e. none of the above

5.   Which of the following countries have had (at some time) labor costs in manufacturing that are higher than in the U.S.?
    a.   Canada
    b.   Japan
    c.   Germany
    d.   all of the above
    e.   b and c

6.   The MRP curve for labor measures the
    a.   extra cost from one more unit of labor.
    b.   extra revenue from selling one more unit of output.
    c.   extra revenue generated by the output of one more unit of labor.
    d.   marginal resource price in world markets.
    e.   none of the above

7.   An extra unit of labor increases output from 10 to 12 units per hour, and each unit sells for $5. What is the MRP of labor?
    a.   1
    b.   2
    c.   10
    d.   20
    e.   none of the above

8.   What is the marginal product of labor in #7?
    a.   1
    b.   2
    c.   10
    d.   20
    e.   none of the above

9.   What is the value for marginal revenue in #7?
    a.   1
    b.   2
    c.   10
    d.   20
    e.   none of the above

10.   What is the maximum wage rate that the firm in #7 will pay?
    a.   1
    b.   2
    c.   10
    d.   20
    e.   none of the above

11. What is the equilibrium value for the wage rate and quantity of labor in the table below?

Wage Rate	$2	$4	$6	$8	$10
Labor Supplied	1	2	3	4	5
Labor Demanded	10	8	6	4	2

    a.   W = $4 and Labor Quantity = 5
    b.   W = $6 and Labor Quantity = 6
    c.   W = $8 and Labor Quantity = 8
    d.   W = $8 and Labor Quantity = 4
    e.   none of the above

12. If the U.S. has relatively more skilled labor and Mexico has relatively more unskilled labor, then what does the factor proportions theory predict will happen if each country specializes and trades along comparative advantage lines?
    a.   Wages for skilled workers will rise in the U.S.
    b.   Wages for skilled workers will fall in Mexico.
    c.   Wages for unskilled workers will rise in Mexico.
    d.   all of the above
    e.   a and c

13. If the U.S. is relatively capital abundant and China is relatively labor abundant, then what does the factor proportions theory predict will happen if each country specializes and trades along comparative advantage lines?
    a.   Wages will rise in the U.S.
    b.   Wages will fall in China.
    c.   Returns to capital will rise in China.
    d.   all of the above
    e.   none of the above

14. What happened in the U.S. from 1950 until 2000 to the wages of college graduates compared to the wages of workers who graduated only from high school?
    a.   They increased from 1.4 to 1.8.
    b.   They increased from 1.1 to 1.5.
    c.   They decreased about 20%.
    d.   They increased only about 10%.
    e.   none of the above

15. Why might unit labor costs be higher in low wage countries than in high wage countries?
    a.   Workers are less healthy in low wage countries.
    b.   Workers in high wage countries have more skill.
    c.   Firms use an inferior technology in low wage countries.
    d.   all of the above
    e.   none of the above

16.   If tariffs and quotas impede trade between a high wage country A and a low wage country B, then what is likely to happen?
    a.   Labor will move from A to B.
    b.   Firms will move from A to B.
    c.   Labor will move from B to A.
    d.   a and b
    e.   b and c

17.   In a poor closed economy, economic growth is likely to be low because
    a.   firms are very productive.
    b.   saving and investment are low.
    c.   consumption is low.
    d.   all of the above
    e.   none of the above

18.   How have some poor countries with low saving rates used the world economy to accumulate capital?
    a.   Borrow from other countries.
    b.   Steal from other countries.
    c.   Attract foreign firms into the poor country.
    d.   all of the above
    e.   a and c

19.   Which type of capital flow into developing countries has been highly volatile?
    a.   those from other developing countries
    b.   foreign direct investment flows
    c.   shorter-term capital flows
    d.   all of the above
    e.   none of the above

20.   What happens to the MRP of labor and employment within the U.S. if foreign competition forces prices down for many products?
    a.   they both fall
    b.   they both rise
    c.   MRP falls but employment rises
    d.   MRP rises but employment falls
    e.   none of the above

Short-Answer Questions

1.   The home countries of immigrants into the U.S. have changed since the 1950s. Where did they formerly come from and where do they come from more recently?

2.   How does greater openness to international trade and investment affect wages in developing countries?

3.   What does empirical evidence suggest with regard to the effects of lower trade barriers on economic growth?

4. Why do labor and capital often move from one country to another?

5. If the U.S. is abundant in skilled labor and capital, then what does the factor proportions theory suggest will happen to the wages of skilled labor, the wages of unskilled labor, and the return to capital in the U.S. if it specializes and trades along comparative advantage lines?

6. How are market wage rates determined?

7. What curve determines the demand for labor curve?

8. What is the name given to the extra revenue generated by selling the output of the last unit of labor?

9. What, in general, happens to the wage rate in the U.S. when more foreign firms produce the same products as in the U.S.? Why?

10. Why has the ratio: (wages of high school graduates) divided by (wages of college graduates) fallen in recent decades?

CHAPTER ELEVEN

Industrial Structure and Trade in the Global Economy — Businesses without Borders

Chapter Overview

Chapter 11 investigates the influence of **market structures** (i.e., the different types of competition that exist in reality) influence international trade and investment. There are four types of market structures, namely: (1) **perfect competition**, (2) **monopolistic competition**, (3) **oligopoly**, and (4) **monopoly**. The last three all fall under the broad category called **imperfect competition**. Monopolistic competition is of particular interest here, because in this market structure many firms compete vigorously, and each firm has a **differentiated product**, i.e., its product is different in some way from the products of other firms in the same industry. This helps to explain why a country might export and import the same product, as the U.S. does for cars. Since home and foreign cars are not identical, consumers have a great variety of choice which they use to buy home and foreign versions of the same product. This is one example of and reason for **intra-industry trade.**

Economies of scale exist if an increase in the size of a firm (and, hence, a larger output) serves to reduce the **long run average cost**. If long run average cost rises with the size of the firm then **diseconomies of scale** exist. The **minimum efficient scale** for a firm refers to that size for the firm that minimizes its long run average cost. These concepts also help to explain intra-industry trade internationally. If the market for a particular type of product, say fuel efficient cars in Japan, is strong, then the firms in that country will grow large enough to experience their minimum efficient scale. This means that the price of this version of the product will be relatively low in that country, which, in turn, might create a comparative advantage in that product. On the other hand, if demand in another country (say, the U.S.) has been strong for a slightly different version of the product (such as larger less fuel efficient cars) then U.S. firms can use economies of scale to obtain a comparative advantage in this version of the product. This helps to explain why the U.S. simultaneously imports and exports cars.

The existence of free trade means that the firms in a small country have the entire world as their potential market. This allows them to grow and take advantage of economies of scale that would not be available if their customers were limited to their domestic market. In general, competition is so strong within a monopolistically competitive market that each firm ends up (in the long run) earning **zero economic profits**, which means that their accounting profits are just equal to the opportunity cost of their being in business. Within an international setting, foreign competition forces home firms to reduce their price in order to keep from losing all of their customers to imports. This eventually leads to zero economic profits for the home firms, and lower prices for consumers.

The fact that consumers in different countries might prefer different versions of the same product helps to explain **horizontal foreign direct investment**. Each firm builds a factory in many countries, with each factory producing a slightly different version of the same product to satisfy the preferences of the population in that country. If there are barriers to international trade, then horizontal foreign direct investment will be larger. The existence of economies of scale in the production of parts to a product (such as the wheels, motors, seats, etc. of cars) induces firms to make all of any one part at a single plant. This generates **vertical foreign direct investment**, which then leads to intra-industry trade as parts for a product are shipped globally.

Firms can enjoy positive economic profits (which means that accounting profit are high) if **barriers to entry** exist. These barriers can take many forms. One is a **first-mover** advantage, which means that the first firm to produce a new product has an advantage because buyers identify this product with the brand produced by the first-mover. Other barriers to entry include: the existence of significant economies of scale, which means that new firms, who are typically small, will have higher per unit costs and prices; the exclusive ownership of a key raw material needed to produce a product; or a **legal monopolies** granted by the government. The latter arises via **patents**, or **licenses** (as is the case with most public utilities).

In an **oligopoly** each of the few firms always takes account of how its competitors will react to its pricing and production decisions, as one does when playing checkers or chess. **Monopolies** always charge a higher price than would exist within a competitive market, which means that monopolies always reduce consumers' surplus. However, monopolies rarely exist unless they are created by government actions, as with public utilities. Nevertheless, if oligopolistic firms get together (collude) and act as though they are a monopoly, then the resulting **cartel** can enjoy high profits until one or more firms within the cartel decides to cheat on its agreement to restrict output.

Dumping occurs if a firm sells its product in a foreign market either at a price below its domestic price or at a price below its cost per unit. Even though dumping helps consumers because they can buy at a lower price, dumping can be a form of **predatory pricing** wherein the dumping is intended to drive all competitors out of business. In this case, the dumping is eventually followed by high monopoly prices.

The degree of competition within a particular market is often assessed via the calculation of a **concentration ratio**, which measures the percent of total product sales that are accounted for by the largest firms (often the biggest three or four firms) within the industry. A more accurate measure of competition is the **Herfindahl–Hirschman index** that calculates the sum of the squares of the market shares enjoyed by each firm in an industry. All calculations that attempt to measure the influence of large firms are complicated by the fact that the **extent of the market** is difficult to define, especially when international trade means the relevant market encompasses the entire world.

Anti-trust laws attempt to prevent firms from becoming monopolies or from forming cartels that act like a monopoly. Such laws often make it illegal for a firm to engage in **price discrimination**, especially when the firm charges a different price for the same product to different customers. Frequently, however, governments engage in some type of **industrial policy** that attempts to help particular industries. Such actions sometimes violate the goals of the anti-trust laws. Finally, a current problem is that different countries, such as the U.S. and EU, have different anti-trust laws, which can give a competitive advantage to the firms located in the country where anti-trust laws are more permissive.

Key Terms and Concepts

Antitrust laws
Barriers to entry
Concentration ratio
Diseconomies of scale
Dumping
Economic profit
Economies of scale
First-mover advantage
Herfindahl–Hirschman index
Horizontal foreign direct investment
Imperfect competition
Industrial organization
Industrial policies
Long run average cost

Marginal cost
Minimum efficient scale
Monopolistic competition
Monopoly
Oligopoly
Predatory pricing
Price discrimination
Relevant market
Vertical foreign direct investment

Multiple-Choice Questions

1. Which market structure has many firms and each one has a slightly different product?
    a. perfect competition
    b. monopolistic competition
    c. oligopoly
    d. monopoly
    e. none of the above

2. Which market structure has a few firms who always consider how their competitors will react to their output and pricing decisions?
    a. perfect competition
    b. monopolistic competition
    c. oligopoly
    d. monopoly
    e. none of the above

3. When a country exports and imports the same product this is called
    a. intra-industry trade.
    b. inter-industry trade.
    c. first-mover trade.
    d. irrational trade.
    e. none of the above

4. If a firm doubles all inputs (and therefore doubles its total costs of production) and finds that its output more than doubles, then what happens to its long run average cost, LRAC, and what name is given to this situation?
    a. LRAC falls and this is an example of diseconomies of scale.
    b. LRAC rises and this is an example of diseconomies of scale.
    c. LRAC falls and this is an example of economies of scale.
    d. LRAC rises and this is an example of diseconomies of scale.
    e. none of the above

5. "Minimum efficient scale" exists when a firm
    a. is as small as possible while still making positive economic profits.
    b. is as small as possible and have low average unit costs.
    c. has the optimum size and minimum average unit costs.
    d. has the most advanced technology.
    e. none of the above

6. In the long run, monopolistically competitive firms have
   a. zero economic profits.
   b. positive but low economic profits.
   c. high economic profits.
   d. negative economic profits.
   e. none of the above

7. Intra-industry trade arises because of
   a. economies of scale.
   b. differentiated products.
   c. the fact that multi-national firms ship parts from one plant to many others.
   d. all of the above
   e. none of the above

8. Suppose that good X and good Y both have economies of scale in their production, and that people in the U.S. strongly prefer X, while people in Japan prefer Y. What do we know?
   a. The U.S. is likely to have a comparative advantage in X.
   b. Japan is likely to have a comparative advantage in Y.
   c. The U.S. is likely to have a comparative advantage in Y, while Japan has a comparative advantage in X.
   d. a and b
   e. none of the above

9. Horizontal foreign investment is when
   a. many foreign firms build the same type of factories in one country.
   b. a multinational firm produces the different parts for a product in many countries.
   c. a multinational firm produces different versions of the same good in more than one country.
   d. a multinational firm imports most of the intermediate products used in a final product.
   e. none of the above

10. A "first-mover advantage" relates to the fact that the first firm to
    a. cut its prices is likely to steal many of its competitors customers.
    b. advertise extensively is likely to enjoy the largest share of the market.
    c. produce a new product gains an advantage because buyers think of its version of the product as being the industry product.
    d. a and b
    e. none of the above

11. If foreign firms engage in dumping in the home country, then this
    a. helps home consumers.
    b. harms domestic producers.
    c. might be a form of predatory pricing.
    d. all of the above
    e. a and b

12.   Which of the following are "barriers to entry"?
       a.   patents
       b.   licenses
       c.   first-mover advantage
       d.   all of the above
       e.   none of the above

13.   If a group of firms get together and agree to act collectively as a monopoly, then this
       a.   is an example of a cartel
       b.   probably violates the country's anti-trust laws.
       c.   is unlikely to last long, because some firms will cheat.
       d.   all of the above
       e.   b and c

14.   What happens to output, Q, price, P, and consumers' surplus if all of the firms in a perfectly
       competitive industry are bought by one firm which then becomes a monopoly?
       a.   They all decrease.
       b.   They all increase.
       c.   Q decreases, P increases, and consumers' surplus decreases.
       d.   Q and P increase, and consumers' decreases.
       e.   none of the above

15.   What does foreign competition do to the elasticity of demand, E, for a monopolistically competitive
       firm's product, and to the long run equilibrium output, Q, and price, P, for the monopolistically
       competitive firm?
       a.   E and Q rise while P falls.
       b.   E and Q fall while P rises.
       c.   They all fall.
       d.   They all rise.
       e.   none of the above

16.   What does vertical foreign direct investment do to the volume of international trade?
       a.   It decreases it.
       b.   It has no effect on it.
       c.   It could conceivable increase or decrease trade.
       d.   It increases it.

17.   A firm increases all inputs by 20% and finds that its long run average costs decrease by 10%. This
       is an example of
       a.   diminishing returns.
       b.   diseconomies of scale.
       c.   economies of scale.
       d.   minimum efficient scale.
       e.   none of the above

18. Firm A has 20% of the sales of cigars; firm B has 15%; firm C has 10%; firm D has 5%; and firm E has 30%. The remaining 30 firms in this industry are all small and together they have 20% of all sales. What is the "3 firm concentration ratio" in this industry?
   a.   0.45
   b.   0.50
   c.   0.80
   d.   0.65
   e.   none of the above

19. What is the "4 firm concentration ratio" in #18?
   a.   0.45
   b.   0.50
   c.   0.80
   d.   0.65
   e.   none of the above

20. In the jet plane industry firm A has 50% of the market; firm B has 30%, and firm C has 20%. What is the value for the Herfindahl–Hirschman index in this industry?
   a.   0.38
   b.   0.25
   c.   0.80
   d.   0.74
   e.   none of the above

Short-Answer Questions

1. What type of market structure exists if one firm owns 100% of the raw materials needed to produce a product?

2. What are the characteristics of monopolistic competition?

3. What are "economies of scale"?

4. What does the existence of monopolistic competition do to the volume of trade, and what name is given to this type of trade?

5. If a firm has the "minimum efficient scale," then what is true?

6. If all inputs for a firm increase by 50% and LRAC decreases of 10%, then what is this an example of?

7. What name is given to the fact that many multi-national firms build plants in different countries, each of which produces one or two components of the final product that are then shipped to the main firm for assembly?

8. What kind of trade is created in #7 above?

9. What is the 3 firm concentration ratio if: firm A has 40% of the market; firm B has 10% of the market; firm C has 5% of the market; and firm D has 20% of the market?

10. What is an industrial policy?

CHAPTER TWELVE

The Public Sector in the Global Economy

Chapter Overview

Chapter 12 explores the international aspects of consumer protection, government protection of intellectual property rights, environmental issues, and government financing of their expenditures. Many people feel that the government should protect consumers, because **asymmetric information** exists. That is, the seller usually knows much more about the product than the buyer does, and, hence, can hide defects or flaws in a product. This is especially important because of **adverse selection**, which means that the sellers of inferior products are the most likely to misrepresent their products. Consumers also need protection because sellers might not keep their promises about after-sale services and warranties, thereby creating a **moral hazard** problem.

In addition to protecting consumers, governments also protect those who develop ideas. That is, governments safeguard **intellectual property rights** by: (a) issuing **copyrights** to the original provider of creative works, including books, articles, software, and video and audio recordings; (b) allowing firms to register and have the exclusive right to use a **trademark**; and (c) granting **patents** to an inventor for a specific (usually extended) period. Society faces a trade-off when dealing with the protection of intellectual property rights. If they were not protected, then others could quickly copy any new idea, which would create competition for the original innovator, and thereby lead to a lower price for consumers. However, if there were no protection of intellectual property rights, there would be little incentive for anyone to spend time and money to come up with a new idea or better product. Thus, the rate of technological and other progress would suffer. Another problem with protection for firms and consumers that has arisen lately deals with how E-commerce trade should be regulated.

An unhindered private market economy is capable of a **market failure**, which means that the market generates price and output results that are not optimal for society. This arises when **externalities** exist. A **negative externality** exists if the private cost of a product is less than the social cost, as in the case if the production of a product pollutes the environment. In this case, governments often take action to decrease the output of such a good, and/or to force the producer to absorb some or all of the social cost. On the other hand, a **positive externality** exists if the private benefit of a product is less than the social benefit, as is true if a person agrees to be inoculated against a highly contagious decease. In this case, governments often subsidize the private production of the good or service, and/or governments can provide the product or service directly.

A **public good** is any good or service that can be consumed by many people at once, cannot be consumed by one person without others also consuming it at no extra cost, and cannot be withheld from a person who has not helped to pay for it, i.e., there can be no **free-riders**. Clean air and clean streams and lakes are examples of public goods. Protection provided by the military is another example. A challenge now and in future years is to find a way to get all nations to agree on government policies toward public goods.

Some environmentalists maintain that an appropriate goal for governments is to eliminate all pollution. However, from an economic point of view this is not an efficient approach. It becomes progressively more expensive to obtain progressively less air or water pollution. At some point the **marginal cost** of pollution abatement could exceed the dollar value of the **marginal benefit** from less pollution. The optimum is to clean up the environment until the marginal cost just equals the marginal benefit, and this is very likely to occur when some pollution still exists.

Some people believe that **globalization** worsens pollution, because multinational firms rape the forests, swamps, and streams in developing countries. On the other hand, others point out that there is a strong positive correlation between a country's standard of living and its efforts to protect the environment. In this case, if globalization raises the standard of living of poor nations, then it might also lead to less pollution.

In general, total **tax revenue** collected by a government is equal to the **tax base** multiplied by the **tax rate**. If a country's tax base shrinks, then the **static point of view** is for governments to increase the tax rate in order to keep their total tax revenue from decreasing. Unfortunately, a higher tax rate can induce citizens to shift where they earn their income, i.e., they can have their income show up officially in countries with lower tax rates. Alternatively, the **dynamic point of view** on this issue is that governments should keep tax rates low for activities that lead to higher rates of economic growth, because growth will increase the tax base.

In order to avoid countries competing for multinationals by offering ever decreasing tax rates for them, some governments have attempted to get others to agree on acceptable values for tax rates. Opponents of this say that such an agreement would create, in essence, a **tax cartel,** which would mean higher tax rates throughout the world. These opponents maintain that it is good for the world economy if countries compete with each other (by reducing tax rates) in order to induce more multinationals to locate within their borders. Such activities, allegedly, force governments to become more efficient in order to operate on a lower budget.

Key Terms and Concepts

Adverse selection
Asymmetric information
Common property
Copyright
Externality
Free-rider problem
Global public good
Intellectual property rights
International externality
Market failure
Merit good
Moral hazard
Parallel imports
Patent
Public good
Tax base
Tax competition
Tax rate
Trademark
Value-added taxes, VAT

Multiple-Choice Questions

1.   Which of the following relates to the fact that sellers usually know more about their product than buyers know?
      a.   adverse selection
      b.   moral hazard
      c.   asymmetric information
      d.   negative externalities
      e.   none of the above

2.   Which of the following relates to the fact that the seller of an inferior product is more likely to falsely represent the product?
      a.   adverse selection
      b.   moral hazard
      c.   asymmetric information
      d.   negative externalities
      e.   none of the above

3.   Which of the following relates to the fact that sellers might fail to keep their agreement about warranties and/or services after a sale?
      a.   adverse selection
      b.   moral hazard
      c.   asymmetric information
      d.   negative externalities
      e.   none of the above

4.   Which of the following relates to the fact that the consumption of some goods and services cost society more than they cost the person who buys them?
      a.   adverse selection
      b.   moral hazard
      c.   asymmetric information
      d.   negative externalities
      e.   none of the above

5.   Which of the following relates to the fact that society sometimes benefits more from the consumption of some goods and services than the benefit to the person who buys them?
      a.   adverse selection
      b.   moral hazard
      c.   asymmetric information
      d.   negative externalities
      e.   none of the above

6.   What is true with regard to goods or services that have a negative externality associated with them?
      a.   The output of this good or service is too high for a social optimum.
      b.   Governments should tax the production of this good or service.
      c.   The social cost of such goods or services exceeds their private cost.
      d.   all of the above
      e.   none of the above

7. The government can give an author the exclusive right to sell a book by
    a. issuing a copyright.
    b. registering a trade-mark.
    c. granting a patent.
    d. all of the above
    e. none of the above

8. The government can give an inventor the exclusive right to sell a new product by
    a. issuing a copyright.
    b. registering a trade-mark.
    c. granting a patent.
    d. all of the above
    e. none of the above

9. The government can prevent others from using the same name for a product as is used by the original supplier of this product by
    a. issuing a copyright.
    b. registering a trade-mark.
    c. granting a patent.
    d. all of the above
    e. none of the above

10. What is or are the characteristics of a public good?
    a. It can be consumed by many people at once.
    b. It cannot be consumed by one person without others being able to consume it at no extra cost.
    c. It cannot be withheld from a person who has not helped to pay for it.
    d. all of the above
    e. a and b

11. What name is given to a person who consumes a public good even though they have not helped to pay for it?
    a. a free good user
    b. a free-rider
    c. a free-loader
    d. a shirker
    e. none of the above

12. What is an appropriate policy for the government if a good or service has a positive externality associated with its consumption?
    a. The government should supply the good.
    b. The government should tax the good.
    c. The government should limit the production of the good.
    d. b and c
    e. none of the above

13.   The optimum amount of pollution abatement occurs when the
    a.   marginal cost of abatement equals the marginal benefit.
    b.   marginal cost of abatement exceeds the marginal benefit.
    c.   marginal cost of abatement is less than the marginal benefit.
    d.   total cost of abatement is a maximum.
    e.   total cost of abatement is a minimum.

14.   Globalization might affect the environment
    a.   positively if it increases standards of living.
    b.   negatively if it increases standards of living.
    c.   positively if it pollutes streams and air.
    d.   a and c
    e.   b and c

15.   What is the value for total tax revenue in a country if the tax base is $10 billion and the tax rate is 20%?
    a. $200 million
    b. $20 million
    c. $2 billion
    d. $2 million
    e.   none of the above

16.   Total tax revenue for a government this year is $100 million, and the average tax rate is 25%. What was the value for the tax base?
    a. $25 million
    b. $50 million
    c. $400 million
    d.   It is impossible to determine with the given information.

17.   If the tax base falls in a country, and the government raises tax rates in order to prevent total tax revenue from falling, then what approach is the government taking, and what is likely to happen to the tax base in the future?
    a.   The static approach and tax base will decrease more.
    b.   The static approach and the tax base will increase or at least stop falling.
    c.   The dynamic approach and the tax base will decrease more.
    d.   The dynamic approach and the tax base will increase or at least stop falling.
    e.   none of the above

18.   If the tax base falls in a country, and the government reduces tax rates, then what approach is the government taking, and what is likely to happen to the economy's economic growth rate and tax base in the future?
    a.   The static approach, and growth and the tax base will increase.
    b.   The static approach, and growth and the tax base will decrease.
    c.   The dynamic approach and growth and the tax base will increase.
    d.   The dynamic approach and growth and the tax base will decrease.
    e.   none of the above

19.   One argument used against the formation of a tax cartel is that
   a.   higher taxes allow governments to help more poor people.
   b.   lower taxes force governments to be more efficient.
   c.   a tax cartel prevents governments from competing for multinational firms via progressively lowering tax rates.
   d.   all of the above
   e.   none of the above

20.   What is true with regard to governments protecting the intellectual property rights of their citizens?
   a.   They never do this.
   b.   They have always done this extensively.
   c.   They are doing this more now than ever.
   d.   They are still not doing this, but there is growing pressure for them to start.
   e.   none of the above

Short-Answer Questions

1.   If governments agree to not compete for multinational firms (by offering them low tax rates) then what does this create?

2.   If the wind blows air pollution caused by country A over to the air for country B, then what is this an example of?

3.   If someone is able to avoid paying local taxes, even though they enjoy the benefits of local police and fire-fighters, and they send their children to local schools, then this person is called what?

4.   Joe knows that the transmission in his old car is about to break, but he sells his car to Eric who has no idea about this transmission problem. What does this illustrate?

5.   If Eric asks Joe how sound the transmission in the old car in #4 is, and Joe lies and says that the transmission is perfect and he knows of no likely problem, then what does this illustrate?

6.   What is the value for the tax rate if the tax base is $400 and total tax revenue is $20?

7.   If a government currently spends $5,000 to decrease the amount of pollution in a lake, and people say that such a decrease is worth $4,000 to them, then what should the government do?

8.   The government in country A increases the tax rate each time that educated citizens leave and move to country B (and thereby reducing the tax base in country A), where tax rates are low. What approach to taxation is each country utilizing?

9.   What is the name given to a good that can be consumed by many people at once, with no extra cost if more people consume it, but it is not possible to stop free-riders from consuming this good?

10.   What condition should be satisfied in order to achieve the optimum amount of pollution abatement?

CHAPTER THIRTEEN

Rules versus Discretion — Can Policymakers Stick to Their Promises?

Chapter Overview

Chapter 13 studies many aspects of government macroeconomic policymaking within the context of a world economy. The **ultimate goals** or objectives of policy can be divided into **internal goals** (such as low inflation, high and ever growing output, and low unemployment) and **external goals** (dealing with exports, imports, capital flows, and the value for their exchange rate). **Mercantilism** is the belief that a balance of trade surplus is a worthy external goal Many countries have mercantilist type policies, i.e., they attempt to stimulate exports and restrain imports.

Economists disagree as to whether it is better to have **discretionary policymaking**, wherein the government actively responds to economic events in order to minimize any negative effects of the events, or **policy rules**, which constrain the government to a fixed strategy no matter what happens. Discretionary policy is more difficult because of three types of **policy time lags**: (a) the **recognition lag**, which means that it takes time for economic data to be gathered and calculated and for the policymakers to realize that something new needs to be don; (b) the **response lag**, which is tied up with the fact that it takes time for policymakers to decide exactly what they want to do; and (c) the **transmission lag**, which deals with the time it takes any policy to exert its full effect on the economy.

Macroeconomic theory and historical experiences both suggest that in the short run there is a tradeoff between temporary increases in output (and, hence, temporarily lower levels of unemployment) and the inflation rate. Higher output means higher inflation, at least in the short run. Hence, policymakers are likely to "split the difference" by having policies that keep output reasonably high and accepting the resulting higher inflation rates. Also, policymakers usually react strongly to stimulate an economy (via expansionary monetary and/or fiscal policies) if unemployment rises to an unacceptable level.

All of this creates an **inflation bias**. Workers push up wage rates, knowing full well that if the higher wages create excessive unemployment, then the government will come to the rescue with expansionary policies. When such policies occur, they push up prices even faster, which often leads to another round of wage increases, etc. If the government announces that it is going to be tough on inflation and not bail out unemployed workers who have forced their wage rates up excessively, then two results are possible. One is that there is **policy credibility**, i.e., everyone believes the government. In this case, wage demands will moderate and the inflation rate will fall.

The other possible result is that no one believes that the government has the resolve to fight inflation. In this case, workers push up wage rates excessively, and when this causes higher unemployment, the government comes to the rescue with expansionary policies, which is just the opposite of what it said it would do. Hence, we get a high inflation rate.

The upshot of all this is that policymakers need to establish **credibility** if they wish to keep the inflation rate low. One way that has been suggested to obtain this is to have **constitutional limitations** on monetary policy, i.e., do not allow the government to increase the money supply rapidly. Alternatively, the government can appoint a **conservative central banker** who dislikes inflation much more than he or she dislikes unemployment. If the central bank keeps the inflation rate low for an extended period, then it will gain **credibility through reputation**. In all cases, a lower inflation rate is apt to exist if there is an

independent central bank, i.e., it can do what it thinks is best for the economy and not what politicians want it to do.

An **international policy externality** exists if the policy actions of one country spillover to other countries. These externalities can be **negative**, as when a government depreciates its country's currency to improve its trade balance, and, unfortunately, deteriorate the trade balances of other countries, which increases their unemployment rates. Alternatively, these international policy externalities can be **positive**, as when a large country such as the U.S. starts to boom in response to stimulative macroeconomic policies, and the U.S. exerts a **locomotive effect** on the rest of the world by increasing out demand for world exports.

The existence of **international policy externalities** often leads to **strategic policymaking**, wherein national policies are formulated in a manner that takes account of how domestic policies will affect other countries. This can lead to **international policy cooperation** via institutions and procedures that allow central banks to share data, research studies, and plans, or it can lead to **international policy coordination**, wherein policy makers get together and simultaneously plan all of their policies. Even though the latter is theoretically superior, it means that each country gives up a little of its **sovereignty**, and it is complicated by the fact that the policymakers in other countries might be **incompetent** or they might have **different opinions** about what should be done.

An **optimal currency area** refers to a geographic area (often encompassing several countries) within which it is best to have either immutably fixed exchange rates or, equivalently, a **monetary union**, i.e., one currency. Theoretically, resources, especially labor, should be highly mobile throughout an optimal currency area. In this case, poor economic conditions in one portion of the optimum currency area will induce unemployed labor to move to more prosperous regions. If labor is not completely mobile, then it is best to allow each region or country to have its own currency so that a depressed country can depreciate its currency in order to become competitive. Most (but not all) of the EU countries have adopted the euro as their currency, even though labor is not perfectly mobile there. Economists anxiously await the results.

Key Terms and Concepts

Bank for International Settlements (BIS)
Capacity output
Central banker contract
Conservative central banker
Discretionary policymaking
External goals
Inflation bias
Internal goals
International policy cooperation
International policy coordination
International policy externalities
Locomotive effect
Mercantilism
Monetary union
Optimal currency area
Policy credibility
Policy rule
Policy time lags
Recognition lag
Response lag

Sovereignty
Strategic policymaking
Structural interdependence
Theory of optimal currency areas
Time inconsistency problem
Transmission lag
Ultimate goals

Multiple-Choice Questions

1. Which of the following is or are **not** internal goals for an economy?
    a. low inflation rate
    b. high level of output
    c. a stable exchange rate
    d. All of the above are internal goals.
    e. none of the above

2. External goals for an economy can deal with desired values for
    a. exports.
    b. imports.
    c. capital flows.
    d. all of the above
    e. none of the above

3. Mercantilists believe that
    a. exports are good.
    b. imports are bad.
    c. a positive balance of trade is desirable.
    d. all of the above
    e. none of the above

4. Which of the following relates to the fact that it takes time for a discretionary policy to exert its full effect on the economy?
    a. response lag
    b. recognition lag
    c. transmission lag
    d. all of the above
    e. none of the above

5. Which of the following relates to the fact that it takes time for data to be gathered, tabulated, and analyzed?
    a. response lag
    b. recognition lag
    c. transmission lag
    d. all of the above
    e. none of the above

6.   Which of the following relates to the fact that it takes time for policymakers to decide if an action should be taken and, then, what the appropriate action should be?
    a.   response lag
    b.   recognition lag
    c.   transmission lag
    d.   all of the above
    e.   none of the above

7.   Which of the following is an example of discretionary policymaking?
    a.   A currency board keeps the exchange rate pegged.
    b.   The central bank must increase the money supply by 6% each year.
    c.   The government's budget must be balanced each year.
    d.   all of the above
    e.   none of the above

8.   If workers push up wages excessively because they know that the government will never allow excessive unemployment to exist for very long, then this creates
    a.   an inflation bias.
    b.   a deflationary bias.
    c.   an independent central bank.
    d.   low interest rates.
    e.   none of the above

9.   Policy credibility exists if
    a.   everyone believes that the central bank is going to be tough on inflation.
    b.   no one believes that the central bank is going to be tough on inflation.
    c.   everyone believes that the central bank will always act to prevent excessive unemployment.
    d.   all of the above
    e.   none of the above

10.   A conservative central banker is one who
    a.   always wears pin-stripped vested suits.
    b.   is a Republican.
    c.   hates inflation more than unemployment.
    d.   hates unemployment more than inflation.
    e.   none of the above

11.   If a central bank announces that it is going to fight inflation, and if it holds to this resolve, but the bank does not have credibility, then
    a.   wages rates will continue to rise rapidly.
    b.   the inflation rate will continue to be high for awhile.
    c.   a recession is bound to occur eventually.
    d.   all of the above
    e.   none of the above

12.   What is the relationship between central bank independence and inflation rates?
    a.   There is a positive relationship.
    b.   There is a negative relationship.
    c.   There is no relationship at all.
    d.   The relationship is sometimes positive and sometimes negative.

13. The time inconsistency problem refers to the fact that
    a.   it takes time to collect data and revisions in the data are often substantial.
    b.   it takes time to make policy decisions and sometimes they seem to contradict each other.
    c.   it pays policymakers to be consistent over time.
    d.   if the government has been tough on inflation and has obtained credibility, it might be advantageous to change their policy unexpectedly.
    e.   none of the above

14. Which of the following represents an example of an international policy **negative** externality?
    a.   The Federal Reserve stimulates the U.S. economy, and we import much more.
    b.   Brazil depreciates it currency, and, thus, imports much less from Argentina.
    c.   The G7 countries have a conference to discuss the economic situation in each country.
    d.   The central banks of the G7 countries agree to sell dollars in the FX market in order to drive the value of the dollar down.
    e.   none of the above

15. Which of the following represents an example of an international policy **positive** externality?
    a.   The Federal Reserve stimulates the U.S. economy, and we import much more.
    b.   Brazil depreciates it currency, and, thus, imports much less from Argentina.
    c.   The G7 countries have a conference to discuss the economic situation in each country.
    d.   The central banks of the G7 countries agree to sell dollars in the FX market in order to drive the value of the dollar down.
    e.   none of the above

16. Which of the following represents an example of international policy **coordination**?
    a.   The Federal Reserve stimulates the U.S. economy, and we import much more.
    b.   Brazil depreciates it currency, and, thus, imports much less from Argentina.
    c.   The G7 countries have a conference to discuss the economic situation in each country.
    d.   The central banks of the G7 countries agree to sell dollars in the FX market in order to drive the value of the dollar down.
    e.   none of the above

17. Which of the following represents an example of international policy **cooperation**?
    a.   The Federal Reserve stimulates the U.S. economy, and we import much more.
    b.   Brazil depreciates it currency, and, thus, imports much less from Argentina.
    c.   The G7 countries have a conference to discuss the economic situation in each country.
    d.   The central banks of the G7 countries agree to sell dollars in the FX market in order to drive the value of the dollar down.
    e.   none of the above

18. Which of the following represents an example of the locomotive effect?
    a.   The Federal Reserve stimulates the U.S. economy, and we import much more.
    b.   Brazil depreciates it currency, and, thus, imports much less from Argentina.
    c.   The G7 countries have a conference to discuss the economic situation in each country.
    d.   The central banks of the G7 countries agree to sell dollars in the FX market in order to drive the value of the dollar down.
    e.   none of the above

19. What is the most important characteristic of an optimum currency area?
     a.   similar tax laws
     b.   similar interest rates
     c.   similar inflation rates
     d.   Labor is mobile throughout the area.
     e.   none of the above

20. Which of the following members of the EU does not have the euro as its currency?
     a.   England
     b.   France
     c.   Germany
     d.   Italy
     e.   All of the above have the euro as their currency.

Short-Answer Questions

1.   Who believes that exports are good and imports are bad?

2.   What name is given to the ability of a government to respond to economic events with the appropriate economic policy?

3.   What do we call the fact that it takes time for an economic policy to exert its full effect on the economy?

4.   In the short-run what is the relationship between inflation and unemployment?

5.   What name is given to the maximum real output that an economy is capable of producing?

6.   If workers push up wages excessively and the government always responds to rising unemployment rates with expansionary economic policies, then what does this create in the economy with regard to prices?

7.   If the government announces that it is going to be tough on inflation, and everyone believes them, then we can say that the government has what?

8.   What will happen to the inflation rate in #7?

9.   What will happen to the unemployment rate in the short run if the government announces that it will be tough on inflation and if it sticks to its resolve, but no one believes it?

10. If one country's government stimulates its aggregate demand and increases its GDP, and this, in turn, prompts an increase in imports that stimulates other countries, then what is this is an example of?

CHAPTER FOURTEEN

Dealing with Financial Crises — Does the World Need a New International Financial Architecture?

Chapter Overview

Chapter 14 deals with financial crises in the world economy, as well as existing international institutions that are designed to prevent them and to mitigate their harmful effects. A **financial crisis** exists when a nation's financial system is unable to function, and such a crisis usually includes a banking crisis, a currency crisis, and a foreign debt crisis. More specifically, many banks go bankrupt, the home currency depreciates significantly, and payments on debts to foreigners cannot be made. In the eight years from the end of 1994 through the end of 2002 there were many financial crises, including Mexico (1994-95), several East Asian countries (1997-98), Russia (1998-99), Brazil (1999), and Argentina (2002). This chapter investigates alternative theories as to why these occurred, including the role played by international financial institutions, such as the IMF, in helping countries who have been in a financial crisis, as well as arguments as to why the IMF's policies could have contributed to these crises. The chapter ends with proposals to alter, or perhaps dismantle, the IMF.

In the decade of the 1990s, international capital flows increased more rapidly than trade flows, which also grew rapidly. These increases have been associated both with foreign direct investment, which is always long term in nature, and portfolio capital flows, which are typically shorter term in nature. One reason for the increase in foreign direct investment (60% of which is among the developed countries) has been a large increase in the number of **cross-border mergers and acquisitions**. Portfolio capital flows increased rapidly as money managers in the developed countries invested huge sums in developing countries in order to obtain high interest rates and expected high rates of return in foreign stock markets.

The large increase in international capital flows during the 1990s was welcomed by economists, because theoretically the free movement of capital internationally will increase world output. To explain, if all of a country's domestic saving must stay at home and be used only for domestic investment, then potentially higher rates of return on investment projects in other countries may go unrealized. The lower rates of return at home will be associated with a lower productivity for capital, and, hence, a lower rate of increase in output. On the other hand, if funds always flow to the country where the productivity of capital and rate of return are highest, then output will grow faster throughout the world.

The free movement of capital internationally also helps to **smooth consumption** over the business cycle. During a booming period, home residents might not wish to consume as much as usual, and, thus, can invest some of their high saving abroad. On the other hand, during a domestic recession, home residents can borrow from abroad in order to help keep their consumption high even though incomes have fallen temporarily. The financial sectors of all economies serve as **financial intermediaries** in that they take funds from savers and channel them to borrowers for consumption and investment.

Although there is still some differences of opinion on the subject, there is a growing consensus that **financial sector development** is a prerequisite for strong economic growth. If the home financial sector is not well developed, then the funds coming into a country via portfolio capital inflows are often used inefficiently. For example, during the 1990s banks in developing countries often had so much money to lend that they lowered their risk standards to precarious levels in order to find borrowers. Also, a poorly developed financial sector (as in many developing countries) cannot withstand an abrupt reversal of international capital flows, as occurs when a few international money managers begin a **speculative**

attack, and others engage in **herding activity**. In such cases, stock and bond prices can fall precipitously, as can the exchange rate value of the home currency, as speculators pull their funds out of the home country.

In the early to mid-1990s vast sums of portfolio capital flows went to developing nations. This is very risky, because such funds can usually be withdrawn quickly. On the other hand, foreign direct investment capital inflows are less easily withdrawn, and, thus, are a safer source of funds for developing countries. There is some disagreement as to whether it pays a developing country to place controls on portfolio capital inflows, such as restricting their value or preventing the funds from leaving the country rapidly without a severe penalty. Chile appears to have had some positive results from such controls, but they are considering dropping them, because the controls induce international investors to place their funds in other countries.

The alternative theories concerning the cause of financial crises fall into two broad categories. Fist, a crisis might be caused by economic fundamentals, i.e., a current account deficit, large government budget deficits, poor quality for bank loans, etc. that induce speculators to rapidly take funds out of a country. Second, a crisis might arise even tough a country's economic fundamentals are sound if the expectations of a crisis become self-fulfilling. That is, if enough speculators believe that a country might soon experience a financial crisis, then their actions can make the crisis occur. This appears to happen most frequently when one country experiences a financial crisis, and then speculators fear that the crisis will spread to nearby countries. This phenomenon is referred to as **contagion.**

The World Bank's main function is to make long term loans for economic development, but it is often criticized for making loans that could have been obtained via private capital markets. Critics argue that the World Bank should lend funds only when private funds cannot be obtained. The IMF's main function is to lend on a short term basis to countries that are experiencing a financial crisis, as defined above. Critics of the IMF say that it does very little to prevent a crisis, and that it sometimes makes longer term loans to poor countries, a function that perhaps should be left to the World Bank. Critics also point out that the **ex ante conditionality** that accompanies loans to borrowing countries is not made public. This makes it easier for the borrowers to cheat on their agreements with the IMF. Then, the IMF often levies more severe **ex post conditionality** that can cause severe hardships. Most economists believe that the actions of the IMF should be made public at all times, and that it should not make longer term loans for economic development, but confine its activities to preventing and mitigating the effects of financial crises.

Key Terms and Concepts

Conditionality
Contagion
Cross border mergers and acquisitions
Early warning system
Economic fundamentals
Ex ante conditionality
Ex post conditionality
Financial crisis
Financial crisis indicator
Financial instability
Financial sector development
Foreign direct investment
Herding behavior
International financial architecture
International Monetary Fund, IMF

Policy-created distortion
Portfolio investment
Special drawing rights
Speculative attack
Quota subscriptions
World Bank

Multiple-Choice Questions

1. What is typically included in a financial crisis?
    a.   a banking crisis
    b.   an exchange rate crisis
    c.   a foreign debt crisis
    d.   all of the above
    e.   none of the above

2. What is the average percentage of total world foreign direct investment that takes place within the developed countries in recent years?
    a.   40%
    b.   50%
    c.   60%
    d.   70%
    e.   none of the above

3. What has happened to the total value of world foreign direct investment in the last decade or so?
    a.   It has risen but less than 100%.
    b.   It has more than doubled.
    c.   It has stayed about the same.
    d.   It increased until 1997 and then it fell sharply.
    e.   none of the above

4. What is an important reason for the increase in foreign direct investment among the developed nations since 1995?
    a.   controls on portfolio capital flows
    b.   decreases in controls on foreign direct investment
    c.   rapid growth of cross-border mergers and acquisitions
    d.   all of the above
    e.   none of the above

5. The free movement of capital internationally is viewed favorably by most economists because it
    a.   prevents financial crises.
    b.   increases output in the world.
    c.   decreases unemployment during recessions.
    d.   all of the above
    e.   none of the above

6. Which of the following countries did not have a financial crisis since 1994?
    a. Mexico
    b. Brazil
    c. Panama
    d. All of the above had financial crises.
    e. None of the above had financial crises.

7. What function do international capital flows perform with regard to consumption and business cycles?
    a. none
    b. Business cycles decrease capital flows and consumption.
    c. Capital flows smooth consumption over the business cycle.
    d. Consumption smooths capital flows over the business cycle.
    e. none of the above

8. According to some economists, how does the development of the financial sector contribute to long run economic development?
    a. It enhances economic growth.
    b. It definitely has no effect on economic growth.
    c. It decreases economic growth because it uses up resources.
    d. none of the above

9. "Herding" refers to the fact that
    a. cattle must be herded in order to keep some of them from going astray.
    b. countries that are geographically close sometimes have a financial crisis move from one to another.
    c. speculators often follow the lead of other speculators.
    d. the stocks of similar countries usually move up and down together.
    e. none of the above

10. "Contagion" refers to the fact that
    a. some serious diseases are contagious internationally.
    b. countries that are geographically close sometimes have a financial crisis move from one to another.
    c. speculators often follow the lead of other speculators.
    d. the stocks of similar countries usually move up and down together.
    e. none of the above

11. "Self-fulfilling expectations" can cause
    a. a financial crisis.
    b. a policy-created distortion.
    c. financial intermediaries.
    d. all of the above
    e. none of the above

12. A "policy-created distortion" exists if government policy
    a. takes the output of some goods away from their optimal values.
    b. distorts our perspective on the economy.
    c. eliminates negative externalities.
    d. all of the above
    e. none of the above

13. Financial intermediaries
    a. help funds that are saved to go to worthwhile investment projects.
    b. match up savers with borrowers.
    c. reduce information asymmetries.
    d. all of the above
    e. none of the above

14. What are some problems that are pervasive to financial markets?
    a. adverse selection
    b. herding behavior
    c. moral hazard
    d. all of the above
    e. none of the above

15. International portfolio investment involves
    a. the acquisition of foreign assets that results in more than a 10% ownership share in a foreign firm.
    b. the acquisition of foreign assets that results in less than a 10% ownership share in a foreign firm.
    c. is typically long term in nature.
    d. a and c
    e. b and c

16. What role did portfolio capital flows play in recent financial crises?
    a. The abrupt increase in funds going into developing countries caused inflation and eventually a crisis.
    b. The abrupt reversal of portfolio capital flows triggered several crises.
    c. Controls on portfolio capital flows destroyed several financial sectors and led to a crisis.
    d. all of the above
    e. none of the above

17. Which of the following is a stabilizing element in developing countries?
    a. foreign direct investment
    b. portfolio capital flows
    c. the lack of funds from the IMF and World Bank
    d. all of the above
    e. none of the above

18.   The primary function of the World Bank is to
  a.   give advice to all countries.
  b.   lend funds short-term to countries with a financial crisis.
  c.   lend funds long-term to countries with a financial crisis.
  d.   control exchange rates in developing countries.
  e.   none of the above

19.   The primary function of the IMF is to
  a.   give advice to all countries.
  b.   lend funds short-term to countries with a financial crisis.
  c.   lend funds long-term to countries with a financial crisis.
  d.   control exchange rates in developing countries.
  e.   none of the above

20.   "Ex post conditionality" refers to actions that the IMF requires from a country
  a.   before granting them a loan.
  b.   in order to prevent a financial crisis.
  c.   after a loan has been made.
  d.   none of the above

Short-Answer Questions

1.   What international organization has as its primary function the making of loans to developing countries in order to increase economic growth?

2.   What do we call the funds that each country deposits with the IMF?

3.   What is the name of the composite currency of the IMF whose value is based on a weighted average of five currencies?

4.   What percentage of all voting power in the IMF does the U.S. possess?

5.   What type of institutions help savers to find borrowers?

6.   What name is given to the set of actions that a country must agree to before the IMF will grant the country a loan?

7.   What is the most stabilizing type of international capital flow to developing nations?

8.   What type of countries are recipients of the majority of foreign direct investment funds?

9.   If a financial crisis is caused by economic events, what name is given to the economic variables that cause the crisis?

10.   What do we call it when a financial crisis spreads from one country to another, in part because of self-fulfilling expectations?

ANSWERS TO QUESTIONS

Chapter 1

Multiple-Choice Questions

1. D	5. E	9. A	13. A	17. A
2. E	6. E	10. E	14. A	18. D
3. C	7. C	11. E	15. C	19. B
4. E	8. D	12. D	16. D	20. C

Short-Answer Questions

1. The increasing interconnectedness of peoples and societies, and the interdependence of economies, governments, and environments.

2. Real sector — is engaged in the production and sale of goods and services.
   Financial sector — is engaged in the sale of financial assets.

3. primarily the currencies of different countries

4. Any two of the following:
   a. Increases income inequality, i.e., the rich gain and the poor either lose or gain less.
   b. Firms from affluent nations abuse poor country workers via low wages and/or terrible working conditions.
   c. The environments in poor nations suffer.

5. If it exports the surplus.

6. Consumers are usually willing to pay more for a good than they have to.

7. Sellers are usually willing to sell at a lower price than they have to.

8. Any two of the following:
   a. It enhances democracy.
   b. It reduces corruption.
   c. It increases world output and standards of living.

9. There will be a shortage which induces buyers to offer to pay a higher price and allows sellers to charge a higher price.

10. If it imports the shortage

Chapter 2

Multiple-Choice Questions

1. E	5. A	9. B	13. B	17. D
2. A	6. A	10. A	14. A	18. B
3. B	7. A	11. C	15. E	19. A
4. A	8. A	12. D	16. E	20. C

Short-Answer Questions

1. There is a finite amount of resources, and thus we must produce less of some goods in order to produce more of others.

2. A curve showing the maximum combinations of two goods for any given amounts of resources that are used efficiently with the existing technology.

3. Its absolute value is equal to the opportunity cost of X.

4. The resources released by the Y industry will not be optimal for producing X. Thus, the cost of X will rise as more of these suboptimal resources are used to produce X.

5. Absolute advantage means that a country can produce more of a good (with a given amount of resources) than another country. This, in turn, implies that the good can be produced at a lower cost (a lower price) at home.

6. Consumers gain because they can buy imports at a lower price, and home producers gains because they can sell in world markets at a higher price.

7. Comparative advantage means that a country can produce a good with a lower opportunity cost than exists in another country.

8. It gains because it gives up producing some good in order to produce one more unit of its comparative advantage good, but then it exports this comparative advantage good and obtains more of the other good than it gave up.

9. Some groups of people within each country are made worse off via international trade.

10. Its output and average standard of living will go up if it specializes in the good or goods where its absolute advantage is greatest.

Chapter 3

Multiple-Choice Questions

1. B	5. E	9. D	13. D	17. A
2. A	6. D	10. C	14. A	18. E
3. C	7. E	11. D	15. E	19. D
4. D	8. E	12. D	16. E	20. D

Short-Answer Questions

1.   the knowledge and skills that workers possess

2.   The human capital content of labor inputs was calculated and used to adjust the capital to labor ratios in U.S. exports and imports.

3.   A relatively capital abundant country will have a comparative advantage in the good that is relatively capital intensive.

4.   The income of the resource used intensively in the export industry will rise and the income of the resource used intensively in the import competing industry will fall.

5.   The relatively scarce resource is harmed and the relatively abundant resource is made better off.

6.   The value of the output of a good minus the cost of the intermediate products used in the production of that good.

7.   Economic growth occurs when a country's ability to produce increases. This represents an outward shift in its PPF, and is caused by an increase in available resources and/or an advance in technology.

8.   If the endowment of a resource increases, then (at constant relative commodity prices) the output of the good that uses this resource intensively will rise and the output of the other good will fall.

9.   Relative capital abundance exists for a country when the ratio of capital to labor, K/L, is higher there than in another country. Relative capital intensity refers to the fact that the ratio of capital to labor needed to produce a good exceeds the ratio for another good.

10.   It will export the relatively labor intensive good Y and import the relatively capital intensive good X.

Chapter 4

Multiple-Choice Questions

1. C	5. B	9. C	13. E	17. C
2. C	6. E	10. D	14. D	18. A
3. A	7. D	11. D	15. C	19. B
4. D	8. C	12. A	16. D	20. D

Short-Answer Questions

1. When the buyers pay all or most of the tax, because the price rises by almost the same amount as the tax.

2. When only a specific quantity of a good can be imported over some time interval.

3. It falls.

4. the redistribution effect

5. an ad valorem tariff

6. a combination tariff

7. It is large enough to affect the prices of products in world markets.

8. quota rent

9. Dumping is when a foreign exporter: (a) sells its exports here for less than it sells them in its own country, or (b) sells its exports here for less than it costs to produce them.

10. Levy a countervailing duty.

Chapter 5

Multiple-Choice Questions

1. C	5. A	9. D	13. E	17. A
2. B	6. D	10. B	14. D	18. C
3. A	7. D	11. E	15. C	19. C
4. C	8. D	12. C	16. E	20. A

Short-Answer Questions

1.   A free trade area is a group of countries that have zero tariffs for trade among them, but can have different tariffs for trade with nonmembers, and do not have the free movement of resources.

2.   U.S., Canada, and Mexico.

3.   Exports from the U.S. to Mexico and two-way trade between Mexico and Canada have increased significantly.

4.   trade diversion

5.   15

6.   The International Trade Commission (ITC)

7.   The WTO gives the offended country or countries permission to charge a countervailing duty on products from the guilty country.

8.   an economic union

9.   free trade area, customs union, common market, and economic union

10.   rules of origin

Chapter 6

Multiple-Choice Questions

1. B	5. C	9. C	13. A	17. D
2. B	6. A	10. A	14. B	18. A
3. A	7. D	11. D	15. B	19. D
4. C	8. C	12. C	16. C	20. E

Short-Answer Questions

1. It is a double entry system. That is, theoretically, each international transaction has two entries, a debit (–) and a credit (+).

2. U.S. international sales require a credit (+) entry, and U.S. international purchases require a debit (–) entry.

3. zero

4. The current account balance is calculated by summing the (balance on goods services and income) with the (net unilateral transfer payments).

5. effective exchange rate

6. The dollar appreciated because it takes fewer dollars to buy a euro.

7. The real exchange rate is $(1 \times 200)/150 = 1.33$.

8. In this situation there is a forward discount on the euro of 5%.

9. Forward market speculators will buy euros forward for $0.95 and hope to be able to sell them later in the spot market at a higher price.

10. Dollars per euro = ($ per pound) x (pounds per euro) = $1.50 \times (1/3) = 0.50 per euro.

Chapter 7

Multiple-Choice Questions

1. C	5. D	9. D	13. D	17. A
2. A	6. B	10. C	14. B	18. E
3. D	7. A	11. B	15. A	19. A
4. D	8. B	12. C	16. D	20. C

Short-Answer Questions

1. They are fixed.

2. It makes long term loans for economic development.

3. The money supply increases rapidly.

4. The money supply will not grow.

5. $35 per ounce

6. the early 1970s

7. Exchange rates have been more highly volatile than anyone anticipated.

8. make loans to countries with exchange rate and/or financial problems

9. This was an agreement in 1985 that governments were going to sell dollars in order to drive the value of the dollar down.

10. Neither is necessarily better.

Chapter 8

Multiple-Choice Questions

1. A	5. C	9. A	13. B	17. A
2. B	6. B	10. A	14. E	18. D
3. C	7. B	11. D	15. B	19. B
4. D	8. D	12. C	16. C	20. C

Short-Answer Questions

1. P = SP*, which means that a typical basket of foreign goods and services sells for the same price in home money as the home money price of home goods and services.

2. undervalued

3. They expect the pound to appreciate by 4%.

4. It converges very slowly, with a half-life of 3 to 7 years.

5. buy euros spot and sell euros forward

6. +0.04, which is a forward premium.

7. $ per peso will fall, i.e., the peso will depreciate.

8. 12%

9. The pound will continue to appreciate for the next week or two.

10. The pound will begin to depreciate.

Chapter 9

Multiple-Choice Questions

1. E	5. C	9. A	13. D	17. A
2. C	6. D	10. B	14. C	18. C
3. E	7. B	11. E	15. A	19. D
4. A	8. E	12. E	16. B	20. C

Short-Answer Questions

1. monetary policy

2. Either the sum of all assets or the sum of all liabilities.

3. lender of last resort

4. M1

5. Sell bonds.

6. Sell bonds or lend less to the private sector.

7. The interest rate rises, because the international reserve component of base money decreases, and this reduces the money supply.

8. GDP deflator

9. Both the price level and output will rise, because the money supply increases, and this reduces interest rates. The lower interest rates induce households and firms to borrow and spend more, thereby shifting the aggregate demand curve to the right.

10. Buy home money with FX.

Chapter 10

Multiple-Choice Questions

1. C	5. D	9. E	13. E	17. B
2. D	6. C	10. C	14. A	18. E
3. E	7. C	11. D	15. D	19. C
4. A	8. B	12. D	16. E	20. A

Short-Answer Questions

1. Initially Europe and Canada; recently Latin America and Asia.

2. They increase.

3. Economic growth increases.

4. There are impediments to trade.

5. Skilled wages rise, unskilled wages fall, and returns to capital rise.

6. At the intersection of the labor supply curve and the labor demand curve.

7. the marginal revenue product, MRP, of labor curve

8. MRP of labor

9. Wages fall because product prices decrease.

10. Increased skills are needed in industry and foreign trade has grown.

Chapter 11

Multiple-Choice Questions

1. B	5. C	9. C	13. D	17. C
2. C	6. A	10. C	14. C	18. D
3. A	7. D	11. D	15. A	19. E
4. C	8. D	12. D	16. D	20. A

Short-Answer Questions

1. monopoly

2. many firms, freedom of entry, differentiated products

3. LRAC decreases as the size of the firm increases.

4. It increases the volume of trade, and this is intra-industry trade.

5. The firm as the lowest possible LRAC.

6. economies of scale

7. vertical foreign direct investment

8. intra-industry trade

9. 0.70

10. Industrial policy refers to the fact that some governments actively promote the development of specific national industries.

Chapter 12

Multiple-Choice Questions

1.	C	5.	E	9.	B	13.	A	17.	A
2.	A	6.	D	10.	D	14.	A	18.	C
3.	B	7.	A	11.	B	15.	C	19.	B
4.	D	8.	C	12.	A	16.	C	20.	C

Short-Answer Questions

1. a tax cartel

2. an international negative externality

3. a free-rider

4. asymmetric information

5. adverse selection

6. 5%

7. Engage in less pollution abatement because the marginal cost exceeds the marginal benefit.

8. Country A uses the static approach and country B uses the dynamic approach.

9. a public good

10. The marginal cost of abatement should equal the marginal benefit of abatement.

Chapter 13

Multiple-Choice Questions

1. C	5. B	9. A	13. D	17. D
2. D	6. A	10. C	14. B	18. A
3. D	7. E	11. D	15. A	19. D
4. C	8. A	12. B	16. C	20. A

Short-Answer Questions

1.   mercantilists

2.   discretionary policy

3.   transmission lag

4.   a negative relationship

5.   capacity output

6.   an inflation bias

7.   credibility

8.   it decreases

9.   it increases

10.   the locomotive effect or a positive policy externality

Chapter 14

Multiple-Choice Questions

1. D	5. B	9. C	13. D	17. A
2. C	6. C	10. B	14. D	18. E
3. A	7. C	11. A	15. B	19. B
4. C	8. A	12. A	16. B	20. C

Short-Answer Questions

1. the World Bank

2. quota subscriptions

3. Special Drawing Rights or SDRs

4. 17%

5. financial intermediaries

6. ex ante conditionality

7. foreign direct investment

8. developed countries

9. economic fundamentals

10. contagion